The New Atheist Denial of History

The New Atheist Denial of History

Borden W. Painter Jr.

THE NEW ATHEIST DENIAL OF HISTORY
Copyright © Borden W. Painter Jr., 2014.

Softcover reprint of the hardcover 1st edition 2014 978-1-137-47767-5

All rights reserved.

First published in 2014 by PALGRAVE MACMILLAN® in the United States—a division of St. Martin's Press LLC, 175 Fifth Avenue, New York, NY 10010.

Where this book is distributed in the UK, Europe and the rest of the world, this is by Palgrave Macmillan, a division of Macmillan Publishers Limited, registered in England, company number 785998, of Houndmills, Basingstoke, Hampshire RG21 6XS.

Palgrave Macmillan is the global academic imprint of the above companies and has companies and representatives throughout the world.

Palgrave® and Macmillan® are registered trademarks in the United States, the United Kingdom, Europe and other countries.

ISBN 978-1-349-50215-8   ISBN 978-1-137-47769-9 (eBook)
DOI 10.1057/9781137477699

Library of Congress Cataloging-in-Publication Data

Painter, Borden W.
    The new atheist denial of history / Borden W. Painter, Jr.
    pages cm
    Includes bibliographical references and index.
                                             1. Atheism—
Controversial literature. 2. History—Philosophy. I. Title.

BL2747.3.P28 2014
211'.8—dc23   2014022211

A catalogue record of the book is available from the British Library.

Design by Scribe Inc.

First edition: November 2014

10 9 8 7 6 5 4 3 2 1

Contents

Preface and Acknowledgments		vii
Introduction: Challenging New Atheist History		1
1	The Twentieth Century	9
2	Europe from 1600 to 1900	45
3	Europe to 1600	77
4	Back to the Present: History In and Out of Bounds	115
5	What's at Stake	155
Notes		171
Bibliography		185
Index		189

Preface and Acknowledgments

In the parlance of the Episcopal Church, I am a "nonstipendiary" priest, meaning my name does not appear on any church payroll. Although I have maintained an active life in my own parish, done Sunday services in many others, and officiated at baptisms, weddings, and funerals, I earned my bread and butter for forty years teaching European history at Trinity College in Hartford, Connecticut. My passion for history springs from the conviction that historical knowledge and understanding form a necessary part of a sound education, especially for those who provide political, intellectual, and cultural leadership in our society. That conviction led me to question the version of history I found in the Big Three of the New Atheists: Sam Harris, Richard Dawkins, and Christopher Hitchens.

My journey into New Atheist history began in 2004 when I spotted a copy of Harris's *The End of Faith: Religion, Terror, and the Future of Reason* on the new book shelf in my local public library. I had just completed my fortieth and final year at Trinity, serving as interim president, and had turned to completing a book manuscript for Palgrave Macmillan—*Mussolini's Rome: Rebuilding the Eternal City*—that came out the next year. I made a mental note to read Harris when time permitted. By the time I got to it, the paperback edition had come out, and Richard Dawkins's *The God Delusion* (2006) had appeared. A year later Christopher Hitchens's *God Is Not Great: How Religion Poisons Everything* became the third volume propagating what had now become known as the New Atheism. All three sold thousands of copies and climbed onto the bestseller list.

These books shocked me not for the strident atheism that I anticipated but for their appalling misuse and distortion of history. The authors all appealed to history for evidence to demonstrate how evil and misguided religion in general was, using European and American history to discredit Christianity in particular. Their version of history managed to get the history wrong and to push interpretations of the past out of step with mainstream historical research and writing. I knew from decades of teaching, writing, and thinking about the past how to recognize bad history when I read it.

My life as a history teacher had taken an erratic course that began in colonial America and ended in Fascist Italy, but one that prepared me well for my journey into the morass of New Atheist history. Back in the 1960s when I set out, specialization and the publish-or-perish environment of universities had yet to trickle down to small, liberal arts colleges like Trinity. My major field for my PhD at Yale was English history from the Tudors to the present, with minors in colonial church history and Renaissance and Reformation Europe. My doctoral dissertation began in England but then focused on the development of the vestries or church boards of laymen in colonial Anglican parishes. My position in the history department at Trinity called for me to teach courses that covered Europe and England from the fourteenth to the seventeenth centuries, as well as teaching sections of a general survey of Europe from the late Roman Empire to the twentieth century, commonly known as "From Christ to Khrushchev."

I took a new turn in the 1970s when our department chairman suggested we each think about teaching in new fields in order to enrich the curriculum. I ventured into modern Italian history, began studying Italian, and by the late 1980s focused my research on Mussolini and Italian fascism. Trinity's undergraduate program in Rome, founded in 1970, and Trinity's Elderhostel programs beginning in 1983 gave me ample opportunity to get to Italy for teaching and other duties as Director of Italian Programs.

In the 1980s, the history department added a required historiography course for majors, focusing on historical methods, schools of interpretation, and the development of history as an academic discipline from the Enlightenment to the present. The course allowed me to cast my historical net more widely than the requirements of growing specialization allowed my younger colleagues. The sum of this experience of dealing with the past over four decades and trying to impart some order and sense to it for undergraduates enabled me to sense that something smelled fishy in the history served up by Harris, Dawkins, and Hitchens. In particular, their constant cries for evidence-based reasoning contradicted their treatment of history, where they ignored the evidence presented by mainstream historians. On that score, they seemed to me no better than others who misused history for their ideological purposes.

I read scores of reviews, articles, and books reacting to the Big Three of the New Atheism. Their treatment of the past got a passing grade by default, while I gave them a failing grade in history. In 2007, I published a short op-ed piece on the subject in the *Hartford Courant*. The nasty responses from those outraged that anyone should pose such a challenge to the New Atheists introduced me to the blogosphere and an awareness of the significance of the Internet in spreading New Atheist history. At that point, I decided to write a book.

Over the next several years while writing, I gave talks on New Atheist history to a variety of audiences in and beyond the academic world. I invariably found interest, with questions and comments that helped me develop my ideas. The resulting book is a case study that I hope may interest colleagues teaching courses on historiography. I also hope that a general audience outside the academy will find of interest a book with something new to say on the controversy engendered by the original New Atheists.

I am grateful for the encouragement I received along the way. Jonathan Elukin of the Trinity College history department gave constant support and invited me to give a presentation of this historiographical case study to his class of history majors. Donald Yerxa, former editor of the newsletter of the Historical Society, *Historically Speaking*, published my article and encouraged me to go forward with the book. Chris Chappell at Palgrave Macmillan was quick to show initial interest and to see the project to its completion. My daughter, Ellen Painter Dollar, gave a critical eye to the full manuscript with many suggestions for improvement. My wife Ann patiently endured my extended obsession with the subject and helped with my frequent inability to master my PC. Any shortcomings are mine. My hope is that the product of my labors will provoke some discussion and debate of the use of history in public discourse.

Introduction
Challenging New Atheist History

> If history reveals any categorical truth, it is that an insufficient taste for evidence regularly brings out the worst in us.
>
> —Sam Harris[1]

No doubt Sam Harris directed his self-confident declaration about history and historical evidence at those who have failed to learn the lessons of history with the same clarity and certitude that he has. But in fact, his abstract appeals to history and evidence-based reasoning fail when measured against the concrete conclusions of mainstream historians concerning the topics he addresses in making his case against all religion throughout all history. *The New Atheist Denial of History* calls him and other so-called New Atheists and their allies to account for failing to take seriously the historical record to which they so freely appeal when attacking religion.

Harris's *The End of Faith* (2004), along with Richard Dawkins's *The God Delusion* (2006) and Christopher Hitchens's *God Is Not Great* (2007), rose to the top of the bestseller lists. The fear of Islamic extremism and the political influence of Christian conservatives motivated the authors and help explain the reading public's interest in their books. The books set off a spate of reviews, articles, and books for and against. Yet in all the controversy, little attention has focused on the historical evidence and arguments the New Atheists present to buttress their case. For them, history furnishes ample evidence for the case against religion and for atheism. They are not alone. The method and substance of their history finds favor with a host of individual supporters, including Victor Stenger, Steven Weinberg, A. C. Grayling Richard Carrier, Hector Avalos, Steven Pinker, and a host of websites, particularly that of the Freedom From Religion Foundation.

The number of Americans who profess atheism or agnosticism or do not identify with any religious community is growing. Many are no doubt attracted to the New Atheism by its apparent rationality. It is reasonable to expect, therefore, a widening base of support for New Atheist history, not least among those entering colleges and universities.[2] Currently, Dawkins draws packed houses when he makes campus appearances. In other words, New Atheist history today extends far beyond the pioneering efforts of Harris, Dawkins, and Hitchens. We can expect that New Atheist renderings of the past will likely grow in popularity.

This book is the first to challenge in depth the distortions of this New Atheist history. It presents evidence that the three authors and their allies ignore. It points out the lack of historical credibility in their work when judged by the conventional criteria used by mainstream historians. It does not deal with the debate over theism and atheism, nor does it attempt to defend the historical record of Christianity or religion more generally. It does aim to defend the integrity of history as a discipline in the face of its distortion by those who violate it.

No excuse comes to mind justifying the New Atheist misuse of history. Sound writing on historical topics lies readily at hand for anyone with an interest in them. Both academic historians and those writing for wider audiences produce a steady stream of well-researched books on virtually every subject imaginable. Most historians avoid specialized jargon in favor of straightforward prose accessible to interested readers. The best accounts of the past combine the narrative of what happened with the analysis of why it happened. The New Atheists love to draw on history, but they show little evidence of having read much of it.

History has a dynamic quality because we care about its meaning for our lives and our identities. The historical profession resembles a debating society. New research and new interests lead to new interpretations that challenge previously accepted views, encouraging yet more debate. That does not mean that any presentation of the past will do. The commonly accepted methods of the discipline call for objectively assessing evidence and then presenting the results in a coherent and convincing fashion. The best historians combine both science and art in the difficult business of seeking an understanding of what we as human beings have thought and done over the centuries.

In the past several decades, historians have opened new fields of study and broken fresh ground on topics such as women, African Americans, immigration, the Third World, and more. They have also tried new methods and approaches that seek to open new avenues to the past. They have made use of new technology to collect and analyze vast quantities of data. New Atheist historiography, however, falls outside these innovations in historical study. I will show that in both method and substance, their history is dated and clumsy, manifesting little to no awareness of what mainstream historians of all stripes have to say on the subjects of interest to them.

The New Atheists constantly claim the high ground of evidence-based reasoning in the tradition of the Enlightenment, yet they fail to heed readily available historical evidence that does not support their views, even when presented by scholars trained in history as it has developed since the Enlightenment. Ideology and a set of predetermined conclusions drive their way of doing history. In method, although not in substance, they have much in common with Holocaust deniers, Glenn Beck's "University," the proponents of the "War of Northern Aggression," and others who rearrange history to suit their own ideological and political positions. The irony at the core of New Atheist historiography lies precisely in their failure to carry out their abstract appeals to reason in the specifics of the history they invoke to make their unrelenting case against the evils of religion.

Some of the New Atheist attack seems fair enough in dealing with the history of Christianity: the hunt for heretics and witches, the violence and bloodshed of religious wars, the episodes of intellectual myopia to support supposed orthodoxy. The history of the Christian Church offers much to criticize on moral grounds, as Christians have often acknowledged in reform movements and self-criticism over the centuries. On the other hand, the version of the Christian past offered by the New Atheists differs markedly from the work of trained historians who have devoted their lives to the study of the same subjects.

Instead of relying on the work of professional historians, the New Atheists and their allies follow their own historical methods and interpretations. They have, in short, gone beyond the boundaries of good historical practice. Unlike those who have pioneered new approaches to history, the New Atheists' historical views gain force through constant repetition without reference to what mainstream historians have produced. There is no other way to explain some of the "truths" declared by one or another of the New Atheists:

> Martin Luther King Jr. was only nominally a Christian.
> Joseph Stalin supported the Russian Orthodox Church.
> Totalitarian regimes are religious because they are political religions.
> The popes ruled medieval Europe.
> Without religion we might have had democracy and the Internet by 1600.
> Religion has been the primary cause of war in history.

In the Holocaust, the Nazis acted as agents of religion.
North Korea's regime is Confucian, not Communist.
John Calvin's Geneva was the prototypical totalitarian state.
Only religion makes good people do bad things.

I will examine the evidence presented by the New Atheists in support of these and other specious historical statements. Many of the New Atheists' secondary sources are dated and of limited value. They cite few recent scholarly books on subjects from the Middle Ages to the Third Reich. They misrepresent some books so that they appear to agree with New Atheist views when they do not. Their concerns over militant Islam and the Christian right hardly justify such carelessness in treating the past. Their highminded moral indignation over the evils of religion do not excuse their manipulation and distortion of the past.

Issues of historical accuracy and the uses of history go beyond academic quarrels to find their way into public discourse. Not surprisingly, history often gets manipulated to fit preconceived political and ideological positions rather than informing and shaping points of view. The New Atheists claim they rise above such manipulation because they base their ideas on evidence, but as I will demonstrate, they fail when it comes to their practice of history. It is reasonable to hold the New Atheists to the standards they constantly set in criticizing others. Why should they not adhere to their own standards of reason and rationality in making the case against religion in general and Christianity in particular?

The stakes are high, for if history exists only as an adjunct to ideology, it has nothing of objective and independent value to teach us. History then ceases to be as an autonomous discipline capable of giving some useful and truthful perspective on the human condition generally and our current state of affairs specifically.

The late J. H. Hexter counseled his fellow historians to obey three commandments: (1) do not go off half-cocked; (2) get the story straight; and (3) keep prejudices about present-day issues out. Mainstream historians commonly follow these or similar guidelines in going about their investigations of the past.[3] In violating all three of these commandments, the New Atheists violate the canons of modern historiography. Their contempt for religion brings them to contempt for history as well. Lacking a sense of history, they write history that makes no sense.

The purpose of this book is to present the evidence that the New Atheists have ignored and to point out the distortions of history presented in support of their collective stance on religion. To put it another way, they may have many reasons to conclude that atheism is true and theism false, but the historical piece of their argument demonstrably fails and lacks the intellectual rigor they supposedly stand for.

Chapter 1 takes up the twentieth century, because the New Atheist mistakes and distortions concerning this era are particularly obvious and egregious. They are what drew me into the subject when I first read Harris, Dawkins, and Hitchens, each of whom made statements about the last century that I knew from forty years of teaching made no historical sense and would never be found in the work of professional historians. As I then dug deeper into their treatment of earlier centuries, a clear pattern emerged that cast a dark shadow over their professed Enlightenment rationality. Then in reading more widely, I found that numerous of their allies followed the same methods and drew similar conclusions. I discovered that New Atheist history stretched far beyond the three bestselling authors to form a widespread network of likeminded believers.

Chapter 2 takes us back to the period from circa 1600 to circa 1900, and Chapter 3 from late antiquity through the Middle Ages to 1600. The final two chapters return to the present, giving an overview and summary within the larger context of current misuses of history by those whose common denominator is producing bad history in the service of politics and ideology. Here we will find the New Atheist way of doing history sadly similar to that of other ideologues hijacking the past for their own purposes. Doubtless the New Atheists would object to being placed in such dubious company, but I will present solid evidence for doing so.

I also juxtapose the New Atheist views with those of mainstream historians by including a section labeled "History 101: New Atheist and Mainstream History" in the first three chapters. Those sections offer basic introductions to given periods one would expect to find in history classes or textbooks, with particular emphasis on topics on prominent display in New Atheist history. These sections furnish some background and context for showing the shortcomings of New Atheist history. Throughout the book, I demonstrate that by neglecting readily available historical writing, the New Atheists offer a version of the past that falls outside the boundaries of acceptable history. I will suggest what they could have and should have done if they had remained true to their Enlightenment beliefs, and why we should care, no matter what personal beliefs we hold. I close with a plea that we, as rational people, should seek common ground in exploring the past to avoid manipulating or distorting it for present purposes. If we want history to inform us and help us make sense of the world we live in, we need to agree on good and acceptable methods for plumbing the past. We may still have profound differences over the meaning of history, but at least we will have solid ground on which to stand as we debate those differences.

CHAPTER 1

The Twentieth Century

> What matters is not whether Hitler and Stalin were atheists, but whether atheism systematically *influences* people to do bad things. There is not the smallest evidence that it does.
> —Richard Dawkins[1]

On August 19, 2000, on the Feast of the Transfiguration, the Russian Orthodox Patriarch Alexis II consecrated the new Cathedral of Christ the Savior in Moscow. It stood on the same spot as the old one and duplicated in every detail the gold-domed original, the tallest Orthodox Church in the world. It was a moment of triumph for Russian Orthodoxy and a sign of its resurrection after seven decades of repression by the Soviet Union.

The press covered the campaign to reconstruct the cathedral from its inception in 1990 and subsequently reported regularly on the rebuilding from 1994 to 2000. In the larger picture, historians have written about the Soviet campaign, initiated by Lenin and made state policy by Stalin, to eliminate religion, targeting all religious institutions but especially the dominant Russian Orthodox Church. Historians' works, from general surveys of the USSR to monographs on religious and cultural policies, tell the story of physical destruction of churches and monasteries, persecution and execution of clergy and believers, and attempts to win Soviet citizens to scientific atheism through such means as museums of atheism housed in former churches and proselytizing by the League of the Militant Godless.

In the face of this well-known evidence, Richard Dawkins, justly appalled by the Taliban's destruction of the Bamiyan Buddhas in Afghanistan, informs us that he does "not believe there is an atheist in the world who would bulldoze Mecca—or Chartres, York Minster or Notre Dame, the Shwe Dagon, the temples of Kyoto or, of course, the Buddhas of Bamiyan."[2] Despite such assurances, the Cathedral of Christ the Savior fell to the Soviet wrecking crews in 1931 as part of a systematic campaign by atheist leadership to destroy Russian Orthodoxy. On the site of the razed cathedral, the Soviet government originally planned to erect a monumental Palace of Soviets, topped by a huge statue of Lenin. World War II prevented that project, and so afterward the space became a huge outdoor swimming pool. The swimming pool replaced the cathedral physically, while spiritually the state sought to replace Christianity with scientific atheism. Dawkins's ill-informed statement turns out to be only one of a long list of false, misleading, and irresponsible historical pronouncements from the Big Three bestselling New Atheist authors: Dawkins, Hitchens, and Harris.

As an historian, Dawkins patently falls short in his knowledge and understanding of Soviet policies and practices toward religion. He reduces the topic of Stalin's atheism to whether it influences his "brutality." Dawkins grants that Stalin, who had spent time in a seminary training for the priesthood, "was scathing about the Russian Orthodox Church, and about Christianity and religion in general. But there is no evidence that his atheism motivated his brutality." Dawkins opines that early religious training might have taught Stalin "to revere absolutist faith, strong authority and a belief that ends justify the means."[3] For Dawkins, Stalin's training as a Marxist revolutionary apparently had no influence on his ideology and policies, an opinion widely shared among New Atheist supporters. By focusing on Stalin's personal atheism, Dawkins avoids any reference to the more obvious and important topic of Soviet state ideology and policies with respect to religion.

The treatment of Stalin's atheism and Soviet policy toward religion gives us one example of what emerges as the pattern of historical judgment offered by Dawkins, Harris, and Hitchens. They ignore the narrative and analysis of mainstream historians while substituting their own reading of the past, which commonly includes showing how religion is the root of all evil or, in the words of Hitchens's subtitle, "how religion poisons everything." Hence Dawkins seeks a possible link between Stalin's early religious training and his later absolutism. In the New Atheist version of the twentieth century, "there is not the smallest evidence" that atheism in any way informed Stalin's policies, although the evidence to the contrary is overwhelming.

The subject we need to deal with is precisely the one of historical evidence. Evidence-based reasoning forms the core of the New Atheist argument that religion has been, is, and always will be responsible for all manner of wrongdoing and evil. This book contends that Dawkins, Harris, and Hitchens ignore or manipulate history in ways that violate the basic canons of historical discourse. They do it in ways that undercut their constant calls for the rational consideration of evidence in constructing arguments and reaching conclusions. They may think they have good reasons for believing that atheism is reasonable, but they make a poor case for including historical reasons among them.

The bloody history of the twentieth century continues to engage historians and the general public as we struggle to understand the reasons for the great clash of empires, nations, and ideologies that left millions of corpses in its wake. Many died at the hands of those who set about constructing new utopian societies. Scores of historians have devoted their research and writing to the last century. The New Atheists ignore the work of those historians and instead have concocted their own version for polemical and ideological purposes. Our first task, then, is to take a closer look at the history of the twentieth century presented by these three and their allies.

The New Atheist Twentieth Century

The New Atheists take an aggressive stand in presenting most of the European past as a demonstration of the woeful effects of Christianity throughout the centuries. They are usually on the offensive. When it comes to grappling with the twentieth century, however, all three become defensive. We sense some discomfort and even irritation at having to cope with the bloody turn of events tied to such leaders as Hitler, Stalin, Mao, Kim Jong Il, Pol Pot, and others. These regimes sought control of all institutions in society and, in the case of the Marxist ones, attempted to repress traditional religion altogether and replace it with state-sponsored atheism. Some readers of the New Atheists' books reacted to this version of the recent past by suggesting that in the twentieth century, atheism may have caused at least some of the immense violence, bloodshed, and suffering of Europe and Asia.

Sam Harris took offense at such suggestions. He thought he had dealt with the problem of atheism and twentieth-century dictators in the original edition of *The End of Faith*. The problem with modern "genocidal projects," Harris argued, came from "rigid ideology" that demonstrated that their perpetrators lacked rationality: "Even where such crimes have been secular, they have required the egregious credulity of entire societies to be brought off. Consider the millions of people who were killed by Stalin and Mao: although these tyrants paid lip service to rationality, communism was little more than a political religion."[4] Apparently religion lay at the root of these crimes carried out by antireligious regimes. Another pattern surfaces here that our three amateur historians will employ: Whatever evil came about in the past must have religion as the root cause or stem from secular ideologies that had religious-like qualities and were carried out by people who refused to be rational.

Harris's historical reconstruction of the twentieth century still did not pass muster with some of his critics. They questioned his analysis of modern genocide so much that he felt compelled to refine further his historical judgments in the "Afterword" of the paperback edition of his book. He found it "depressing" to have this question thrown at him, since he had anticipated it and so answered it in the original edition. "While some of the most despicable movements in human history have been explicitly irreligious, they were not especially rational," Harris reiterated. These regimes pronounced "litanies of delusion" about race, economics, nationalism, the march of history, and more, but "Auschwitz, the gulag, and the killing fields are not examples of what happens when people become *too critical of unjustified beliefs*; to the contrary, these horrors testify to the dangers of not thinking critically enough about specific secular ideologies." The problem stems from *dogma*, apparently including secular dogma. "The problem I raise in the book is none other than the problem of dogma itself—of which every religion has more than its fair share. I know of no society in human history that ever suffered because its people became too reasonable."[5] Notice Harris's ploy in linking dogma to "every religion." Harris offers a confusion of categories as he shifts back and forth between the religious and the secular, dogma and reason. It fails to occur to him that some dogmas may stem from secular, not religious, sources. That failure impedes a historical understanding of modern history. It leads to confusion, not clarity, in grappling with the twentieth century.

Christopher Hitchens, fortified with the previously published books of Harris and Dawkins, joined the effort to make religion culpable in twentieth-century crimes. He interjected his own historical understanding of what went wrong in the twentieth century. He does, however, break ranks with Dawkins by readily admitting, "Communist absolutists did not so much negate religion, in societies that they well understood were saturated with faith and superstition, as seek to *replace* it," although he omits the gory details of how such policies of replacement were carried out.[6] He does go on to talk about Stalin's assault on the "museums of Russian orthodoxy," the revolutionary creed of Fidel Castro, liberation theology (which he does not like), and the assassination of Archbishop Romero of El Salvador, "a man of courage and principle," while admonishing the papacy for not condemning fascism and Nazism as clearly as it did liberation theology.

Moving right along, Hitchens informs us that "in a very few cases, such as Albania, Communism tried to extirpate religion completely and to proclaim an entirely atheist state." At this point it is not clear if Stalin's Russia or Mao's China belong among these "very few cases" or whether he thinks that these regimes sought only to extirpate religion partially. But then, miraculously, the religious impulse had once again grabbed hold of these antireligious regimes because "there is nothing in modern secular argument that even hints at any ban on religious observance," and he quotes Sigmund Freud on the "religious impulse." Therefore, he concludes that "all that the totalitarians have demonstrated is that the religious impulse—the need to worship—can take even more monstrous forms if it is repressed. This might not necessarily be a compliment to our worshipping tendency."[7]

Hitchens visited North Korea and found it a pretty stifling place. After describing it in Orwellian terms, he concludes that "students of the subject can easily see that what we have in North Korea is not so much an extreme form of Communism—the term is hardly mentioned amid the storms of ecstatic dedication—as a debased yet refined form of Confucianism and ancestor worship." Once again it is beginning to look a lot like religion. When Hitchens left the country, it was with a "sense of mingled relief, outrage, and pity so strong that I can still summon it. I was leaving a totalitarian state and also a religious one."[8]

By the way, Hitchens adds, "let us admit at once that some of the bravest of these resisters [to the regime] are fundamentalist Christian anti-Communists." Nevertheless, these poor folks preach their deluded gospel to people who have had enough of savior figures. That allows him to launch into an attack on Sun Myung Moon and the "intelligent design" racket, concluding with a reference to the "Burned Over District" in upstate New York during the Second Great Awakening in the early nineteenth century. Lurching forward, he tells us that religion has to admit it is proposing a "total" solution so it must be totalitarian, just as secular, totalitarian political regimes must be religious.[9] Confusion reigns as Hitchens piles one *non sequitur* on another.

Harris views North Korea in similar fashion. The North Koreans have become "utterly deranged by their political ideology," although he does not show any interest in exploring that ideology and its origins. Instead he rails at the North Koreans for their worship of their leaders and becoming a nation now "like a cargo cult armed with nuclear weapons." His analysis of this sad state of affairs begins and ends with such statements as "the problem with North Korea is, first and foremost, a problem of the unjustified (and unjustifiable) beliefs of North Koreans."[10]

Meanwhile, Hitchens admits that "emancipation from religion does not always produce the best mammal either." The scientist J. D. Bernal venerated Stalin and defended his crimes, while H. L. Mencken bought into "social Darwinism" that "included eugenics and a contempt for the weak and sick" and had a soft spot for Hitler. Have no fear, however, for Humanism can correct such errors as opposed to "totalitarian systems, whatever outward form they may take, [that] are fundamentalist and, as we would now say, 'faith based.'"[11] Hitchens thus strains to demonstrate the truth of his subtitle that "religion poisons everything" by the simple device of defining everything that is poisonous as religious.

Last but not least, our three historians agree that Hitler and his crimes belong in the religious camp. Dawkins manifests no interest in probing Hitler's racial ideology per se. Rather, he concentrates on showing that Hitler did not profess atheism and that Hitler and the Holocaust had links to Roman Catholicism. Hitler, he rightly points out, considered himself an agent of "Providence," sent to fulfill a mission. Born a Catholic, Hitler never formally renounced the faith.[12] Dawkins presents several quotations of Hitler, Rudolf Hess, Josef Goebbels, and others to suggest the Führer's ties to Catholicism. He admits that Hitler may have faked any regard for Christianity, but the key point is that he, unlike Stalin, was probably not an atheist and, in any case, "individual atheists may do evil things but they don't do evil things in the name of atheism."

The evil Stalin and Hitler accomplished came from their misbegotten and dogmatic ideologies—ideologies that Dawkins, like his cohorts, does not bother to probe. Confident he has demonstrated the innocence of atheism in these appalling matters, Dawkins concludes his chapter by reminding us that "religious wars really are fought in the name of religion, and they have been horribly frequent in history," although that avoids the question of whether these twentieth-century conflicts stemmed from religion or some other sources, even secular sources. Dawkins never does present informed historical examples of those "horribly frequent" religious wars that have plagued history, and he remains content to offer sweeping, unsubstantiated generalizations. He quotes an illuminating thought from Sam Harris's *The End of Faith* reminding us in no uncertain terms that religious faith "allows otherwise normal human beings to reap the fruits of madness and consider them *holy.*" Besides, Dawkins concludes, no one could possibly go to war in the name of atheism, as it is "an *absence* of belief."[13] The possibility that conflict and war might occur for reasons more secular than religious does not get into the discussion.

The one historian Dawkins cites in his seven pages on Hitler is the late writer John Toland. Toland wrote a popular biography of Hitler that appeared in 1976, *Adolf Hitler*. The paperback edition of 1991, apparently the one used by Dawkins,[14] added a subtitle: *The Definitive Biography*. That claim stretches credulity, for there is no "definitive biography" of Hitler; recent decades have spawned major works based on evidence and sources far beyond anything used by Toland. Anyone today wishing to write intelligently about Hitler would profit from sampling this historical literature.

Toland himself later admitted that "I've learned that the writing of history can never be definitive." He made this remark as a featured speaker at the Tenth International Revisionist Conference on October 14, 1990, in Washington, DC. His speech appeared subsequently in *The Journal of Historical Review*.[15] The Institute for Historical Revision (IHR) that sponsored the conference and published the journal is to this day the leading organization dedicated to Holocaust denial. Toland's biography of Hitler included coverage of the "Final Solution" and the systematic killing of between five and six million Jews.[16] One cannot tell from his speech whether he understood who had invited him to speak, although he should have. His most controversial book, *Infamy, Pearl Harbor and Its Aftermath* (1982), presented the attack on Pearl Harbor as a conspiracy led by FDR. That may have been enough for the IHR to invite Toland, as it favored the notion that FDR conspired to bring about the Japanese attack that allowed the United States to enter the war. That sort of "revisionism" fits well with the argument against the reality of the Holocaust and in favor of the vast conspiracy led by the Jews and the State of Israel to make us think it happened. Toland died in 2004. The IHR web page carried an obituary that stated, "John Toland supported the work of the Institute for Historical Review," citing his lecture to the group in 1990.[17]

John Lukacs in his *Hitler of History* comments that "Toland's admiration for Hitler seeps through in many of his pages, and his documentation, too, is inadequate."[18] As we shall see, Toland gains frequent citation from a number of New Atheist allies and supporters. There are better historians than John Toland to rely on when it comes to making statements about Adolf Hitler.[19] Unfortunately, the New Atheists commonly use as evidence dated or second-rate sources while avoiding more recent and more credible work by major scholars.

Dawkins came across Toland in the two articles he cites from the website of the Freedom From Religion Foundation of Madison, Wisconsin, one of the major atheist organizations. Both articles appeared in the newsletter *Freethought Today*. The first, written by Richard E. Smith, appeared in 1997 and consists of a list of 45 quotations and miscellaneous reflections to show that Hitler's beliefs, inspiration, and actions came out of Christianity. Seven of Smith's points cite Toland's book as the source. He also cites mainstream historians including Alan Bullock, whom he constantly refers to as "Bulluck," and Joachim Fest. Smith presents all his ideas as so many bullet points without any context. Smith identified himself at the time as a student of World War II for more than twenty years, currently working in the entertainment industry and celebrating thirty years as a member of the International Alliance of Theatrical Stage Employees. He was approaching "the various community colleges and universities" in his area with offers to give lectures on Hitler and religion. The second article comes from the foundation's founder and leader, Anne Nicol Gaylor, in August 2004. She makes the case that Hitler lived his whole life as a Catholic, backing up her portrait of Hitler's religious life with quotations from John Toland.

The New Atheists strain to present totalitarian regimes as religious. Harris, for example, manages to imply that Hitler's movement has the qualities of religion in the several pages he devotes to the Holocaust.[20] The device is a simple one: Arbitrarily drop in religion whenever it suits your purpose, as in "Beyond the abject (and *religious*) loyalty to Hitler, the Holocaust emerged out of people's acceptance of some very implausible ideas." Then add the word *dogma*, apparently meant to imply religious or religious-like dogma: "At the heart of every totalitarian enterprise, one sees outlandish dogmas, poorly arranged, but working ineluctably like gears in some ludicrous instrument of death."[21] He offers the conclusion, "The anti-Semitism that built the crematoria brick by brick—and that still thrives today—comes to us by way of Christian theology. Knowingly or not, the Nazis were agents of religion."[22] The assertion that Hitler and the Nazis acted as agents for someone else, let alone "religion," will surprise historians of the Third Reich.

Harris also mixes in the role of the Catholic Church in a way that "merits a slight digression" into the controversy over "modernism" in the late nineteenth and early twentieth centuries. Pope Pius X condemned modernism in 1907. That allows Harris to mention the Index of Prohibited Books. Harris then admonishes the papacy for adding Descartes to the list in 1948 instead of finding "greater offense with which to concern itself," such as, presumably, the evil deeds of Nazism: "Although not a single leader of the Third Reich—not even Hitler himself—was ever excommunicated, Galileo was not absolved of heresy until 1992."[23]

Harris's conclusion to the chapter explicitly blames the Christian faith for a "catalog of horrors" that includes Auschwitz. Once again this version of history points to only one root cause of the evils of the past—religion—and one root cause of Nazism and the Holocaust: Christianity. Such a conclusion would mark a major departure from how historians have explained the Holocaust, if Harris could present convincing evidence for it, which he does not.

Hitchens sets his portrayal of Hitler within the context of his discussion of totalitarianism. He begins by quoting George Orwell: "*A totalitarian state is in effect a theocracy*, and its ruling caste, in order to keep its position, has to be thought of as infallible."[24] Next he tells us that totalitarianism has been around for a long time, since "the early days of mankind." Protestant reformer John Calvin established a "prototypical totalitarian state" in sixteenth-century Geneva.[25] Then, jumping back into the twentieth century, Hitchens further identifies totalitarianism with religion by citing the anti-Communist book of essays by former Communists, *The God That Failed* (1949), a curious misreading of that important product of the Cold War. He then informs us that even earlier Bertrand Russell had spotted the dangers of Bolshevism, although the Church of England had not.

Rather than delve deeper into the origins and characteristics of modern totalitarianism, Hitchens asks the question, "How did religion confront the 'secular' totalitarianism of our time?" Thus he puts religion, not totalitarianism, on trial and uses quotation marks to suggest that totalitarianism may not be secular at all.

In the following pages on Hitler, Hitchens spells out the charges against German Christians, Protestant and Catholic, as enablers of Hitler. He singles out Pope Pius XII for special condemnation, declaring him "pro-Nazi." His notes fail to cite major and important books on the Nazi regime's relationship to the churches and, more particularly, on the controversy over what Pius XII did or did not do in response to Hitler and the Holocaust. The one book he cites, John Cornwell's *Hitler's Pope* (1999), offers a harsh assessment of Pius, although it falls short of declaring the "Vatican's endorsement of Nazi Germany," as Hitchens alleges it does.[26] We will continue to encounter examples of the New Atheist historians distorting the substance of books they present as evidence for their conclusions.

Hitchens excludes any discussion of Hitler's racial ideology and its roots unless he can connect them to Christianity. That follows the method of all three of our historians in selecting only the evidence they believe supports their purposes. They occasionally cite a Christian who lived up to their moral standards. In the case of Nazi Germany, Hitchens acknowledges Dietrich Bonhoeffer and

Martin Niemoller as among the few who opposed Hitler. Even here he cannot bring himself to mention their Christian convictions in that matter, stating that they "acted in accordance only with the dictates of conscience."[27]

Hitchens cites only one book on totalitarianism, what he calls "the magisterial examination of the totalitarian phenomenon," which is Hannah Arendt's *The Origins of Totalitarianism*, published in 1958. He looks in particular at her treatment of anti-Semitism and the centuries of Christian persecution of the Jews, up to and including the Dreyfus case. His point is to connect "religion, race and totalitarianism"[28] in such a way that it avoids the possibility of secular beliefs having any part in the totalitarian mix. His discussion of totalitarianism[29] deviates considerably from what more recent historians have had to say on the subject,[30] but that allows him to concentrate on religion as the historical source from time immemorial of what he defines as totalitarian. Monarchies of China, India, and Persia, empires of Aztecs and Incas, the medieval courts of Spain and Russia, and Calvin's Geneva all qualify as totalitarian, and religion legitimized all of them.[31] Hitchens's totalitarian tent has much larger dimensions than those of historians of the subject. No doubt he has his own unique definition of the term *totalitarian*, but he does not choose to share it with his readers.[32]

As he rambles on, Hitchens throws in personal anecdotes, such as the uncle who had his life ruined by religious fanatics, a reference to Hawthorne's *The Scarlet Letter* to show the connection he makes between totalitarian rule and sexual repression, and sweeping generalizations such as "In the early history of mankind, the totalitarian principle was the regnant one."[33] The fact that contemporary scholars see totalitarianism as a modern phenomenon escapes Hitchens because he has not bothered to read them. In his historical exploration of totalitarianism, one is reminded of the professor's comment on a student's term paper: "This paper is both original and true. The problem is that the parts that are original are not true and the parts that are true are not original." Hitchens again misses an opportunity to explore an important topic, opting instead to continue his polemic that "religion poisons everything."

As he ranges beyond European history, Hitchens demonstrates, once again, his skill at historical manipulation. He takes the opportunity to bring in the "other most hateful dictatorship of the twentieth century: the vile system of apartheid in South Africa."[34] He correctly holds up the ideology of racial separation championed by the ruling Boer National Party and its support by the Dutch Reformed Church. Absent are any references, however, to religiously inspired opposition to apartheid among a minority of Dutch Reformed clergy and laity. Religious leaders such as Desmond Tutu and Trevor Huddleston of the Anglican Church, or Beyers Naudé of the Dutch Reformed Church, as well as other Christian leaders of the antiapartheid struggle get erased from this picture of twentieth-century South Africa, rather like Stalin removing Trotsky from photographs of the Bolshevik Revolution. Standard histories of South Africa offer more complete context that includes the important role of South African, European, and American religious groups in the battle to bring apartheid to an end and to begin a new South Africa.[35]

An outstanding example of Hitchens's revising and manipulating history for his polemical purposes comes with his presentation of another major figure of the twentieth century: Martin Luther King. Apparently offended that Rabbi Abraham Heschel responded to King's leadership on civil rights by likening him to one of the prophets of Israel, Hitchens gives us his own reading of King and Christianity that reaches this remarkable conclusion concerning Martin Luther King: "In no real as opposed to nominal sense . . . was he a Christian."[36]

The collective view of these three authors presents a historical rending of the twentieth century like no other I know. It commits errors of both omission and commission by the selective use of evidence that skews, distorts, and, at times, misrepresents the past. It plays fast and loose with definitions of *religion, secular, dogma, rational, evidence*, and other words central to the subject they choose to treat. Chronology is often hazy, context is commonly narrow, and nuance absent. These shortcomings produce history that would earn a failing grade in an introductory course in modern European history.

History 101: New Atheist and Mainstream History

The distorted history of the twentieth century need not detain us if it were confined to these three bestselling authors, but further investigation reveals a wide network of opinion in print and on the Internet that supports the New Atheist historiography of the twentieth century. Historians of the twentieth century who devote themselves to research and writing for both scholarly and general audiences offer a different version of the last century.

Through a combination of polemical zeal and ignorance, Dawkins, Harris, and Hitchens get history wrong. They claim to marshal evidence that proves religion morally culpable of the greatest crimes of the century. The Big Three and their allies concentrate much of their attention on fascism, Nazism, and communism, without having read what mainstream historians have to say about these subjects.

The term *fascism* originated with the movement, party, and government of Benito Mussolini. In the 1930s during the Spanish Civil War (1936–39), fascism became the generic label for Hitler's Nazi regime as well as Mussolini's and other movements that resembled or emulated these two. Mussolini gained prominence as a radical socialist. He began his migration to the right at the beginning of World War I. Initially Italy stayed out of the conflict; the Italian Socialist Party opposed getting into the war in accordance with socialist doctrine that the true war lays between the working class and the bourgeoisie. When Mussolini joined a chorus of interventionists, the party expelled him. In May 1915, Italy entered the war on the side of France and Great Britain. Mussolini founded the fascist movement in 1919 with a program that mixed extreme nationalism with left-wing goals that included women's suffrage. Political paralysis, economic stagnation, and the perceived threat of a Bolshevik-style revolution gave the Fascist Party an opening on the national stage. When the Fascists staged their so-called March on Rome in October 1922, King Victor Emmanuel III gave in to mounting pressure to accommodate them and bring stability to the country by appointing Mussolini prime minister in a coalition government. By 1926, Mussolini had turned his regime into a one-party state with himself as the infallible leader, or the Duce. Antifascists introduced the term *totalitarian* in describing Mussolini's rule, but the Duce gladly adopted it as a positive label for Fascist Italy. Historians and political scientists subsequently adopted the term *totalitarianism* to describe twentieth-century regimes employing modern technology and media in an unprecedented attempt at state control of society. The New Atheist indiscriminate use of the term *totalitarianism* goes beyond the boundaries of responsible historical practice.

Mussolini proudly hailed his "Fascist Revolution" that would somehow reconcile socialism and nationalism. In practice, he moved to the right to assure the monarchy, the army, the church, and industry that they had nothing to fear from his revolution. He promised to unify Italians as never before and make Italy a strong and respected power.

In regard to these goals, two events stand out. First, the Lateran Accords of 1929 for the first time reconciled the Italian state with the papacy, recognizing the sovereignty of the Vatican state and making Catholicism Italy's official religion. Second, the conquest of Ethiopia in 1935–36 gained wide support within Italy, despite its condemnation by the League of Nations.

Adolf Hitler, like Mussolini, fought in the Great War. Frustrated as an artist before the war, he found a new calling in politics afterward. He quickly established himself as a leader of the new National Socialist or "Nazi" Party. In 1923, he led an unsuccessful coup in Munich against the new German Republic, which landed him in jail for a brief and relatively comfortable time, where he wrote his world view in the book *Mein Kampf*.

Hitler admired Mussolini. He perceived him as an inspired leader whose principles resembled his. The Duce's tactical brilliance gave him a path to power through legitimate means, a lesson Hitler employed a decade after the March on Rome. The Nazi Party also promised a "new order" that would overcome the petty differences of the various parties in Weimar Germany, each of them representing the interest of one group or another. National Socialism promised a unified German nation by establishing a *volkisch* community of racial purity. The Nazi message failed to garner many votes in the elections throughout the 1920s, but all that changed with the onset of the Great Depression and mass unemployment.

In the elections of 1930, the Nazi Party emerged as a major force on the national political scene. By 1932, it gained 44 percent of the parliamentary vote and became Germany's largest party. The government appeared paralyzed and unable to form a viable governing coalition. In the last fully free elections in November, the Nazis lost seats and their percentage of voters dropped to 37 percent, causing a crisis within the party. Hitler's adroit tactical sense led him to hold out for the position of chancellor while reassuring conservatives that he would act as a bulwark against the threat of Communists and Social Democrats. Franz von Papen of the Catholic Center Party offered to form a conservative coalition government with Hitler as chancellor and himself as vice-chancellor. He reasoned that this move would tame the Nazis and put them under the influence of the political right, thereby stabilizing the country. He miscalculated. It was Hitler who would use the conservatives rather than the other way around.

Hitler seized the opportunity to use his constitutional legitimacy to transform his coalition government into a one-party state within 18 months. He skillfully played on both the hopes and fears of politicians to bring new life to the nation by cancelling the threat of a revolution from the left while promising strong and decisive leadership for a new national community for all Germans, from farmers and workers to industrialists and aristocrats, except of course for the Jews. Some violence was necessary, some of it directed against the more radical elements of his own party as a way of reassuring the army and businessmen.

The Nazi road to totalitarianism began with a process known as *gleichschaltung*, a kind of coordinating or bringing together of major institutions into an alignment with the Nazi party and state. The ultimate realization of the new national and racial community envisaged by Hitler would mean an end to any degree of autonomy for government agencies, the military, the press, private organizations, and even the churches.

Hitler took care not to threaten the churches directly. He knew that church leaders, Catholic and Protestant, largely sympathized with his conservative nationalism and charismatic leadership that would bring stability to Germany and put an end to the threat of a Bolshevik-style revolution. He negotiated a concordat with the Vatican that gave the German Catholic Church, to which about one in every three Germans belonged, certain protections and guarantees. The chief papal negotiator, Cardinal Eugenio Pacelli, would become Pope Pius XII in 1939. Hitler then tried to entice the Protestants, about two in every three Germans, into a newly unified German Evangelical "Reich" Church that would endorse an anti-Jewish theology. Despite the appointment of a Reich Bishop and attracting many church leaders, this initiative also spawned some resistance among a minority of Protestants who formed an alliance known as the Confessing Church. Its members included Martin Niemoller and Dietrich Bonhoeffer.

The New Atheists ignore the Nazi attitude toward Christianity, which ran from plans to co-opt the churches for Nazi purposes to hopes of one day eliminating it altogether. Hitler sought to win over Catholics and Protestants immediately after he came to power, but others, like the ideologue Alfred Rosenberg, hoped to transform traditional German Christianity into a new Germanic, race-based religion. For Rosenberg and those Nazis who agreed with him, Nazism needed to replace Christianity once and for all. His book, *The Myth of the Twentieth Century*, proved too long and dense even for Hitler to read. It only became a bestseller after Cardinal Faulhaber condemned it publicly and it was placed on the church's Index of Prohibited Books.[37] Overall, "the historiography of fascism and religion during the last 40 years has clearly established that the leaders of German National Socialism and Italian Fascism were fundamentally anti-Christian, even if, in the latter case, that tendency was more latent than actual during the early stages."[38] The New Atheists ignore or are unaware of this historiography, and they stick to their preoccupation with showing fascism and Nazism as falling in the religious camp.

Germany's stunning victories in France and then in Russia set the stage for Hitler's war against the Jews. The Nazi vision of a racially pure society in the future meant exterminating their archenemies, the Jews, and subordinating inferiors such as the Slavs. The Holocaust took advantage of traditional Christian anti-Semitism but went beyond it. Instead of the Christian goal of eliminating Jews through conversion to Christianity, the Nazi interest aimed for the physical destruction of the Jews, whose survival would mean the constant threat of racial pollution. SS Leader Heinrich Himmler told his men that the work of elimination was difficult, but they had to do it for the greater good.

Nazi ideology included "racial science" that sought to demonstrate a scientific basis for a hierarchy of races. The Nazis did not invent the so-called science of eugenics, which already had widespread currency in Europe and the United States. The Nazi version of eugenics justified their campaign to eliminate Jewish influence and ultimately the Jewish "race." Dr. Mengele and other Nazi doctors carried out their infamous medical experiments in the name of science.

New Atheist accounts of Hitler and the Holocaust have nothing to say about the scientific and pseudoscientific basis of Nazi racism. The point here is not to blame "science" for these horrors but rather to argue for providing the necessary context within which to understand the barbarities of Nazism. The historian's task is that of seeking such understanding, not playing a moralistic "blame game" in the service of an ideology.

Historical controversy has swirled around the role of Pope Pius XII (1939–58) during the Holocaust. Some critics argue that he could have and should have done more to oppose the Nazi assault on the Jews. Defenders of Pius argue that any direct confrontation with the Germans would have violated papal neutrality and brought about German retaliation, including the occupation of the Vatican. Catholic institutions, including those in Rome with direct ties to the papacy, did protect many Jews. Pius made an oblique reference to Jewish suffering and persecution in his Christmas message of 1943. Pius, as Cardinal Eugenio Pacelli, had followed a diplomatic career, and his actions, or lack thereof, bespoke a caution more typical of a diplomat than a martyr. For two decades he and others in the Vatican had contended with the overt persecution of all religious institutions and practices in the Soviet Union, and thus they considered it the primary enemy.

A core ambiguity of the Allied cause in World War II arose from the alliance of the two leading Western democracies, the United States and Great Britain, with the totalitarian Soviet regime led by Josef Stalin. Stalin had managed to outmaneuver all his Bolshevik colleagues following Lenin's death in 1924 to become the undisputed leader of the USSR by the early 1930s. He then sought to eliminate all those he identified as enemies of the revolution.

The enemies Stalin persecuted came not from racial inferiors but from the groups and classes found guilty of exploiting the proletariat or undermining the Soviet party and state, the incarnation of the revolution. When the state began confiscating farmland, collectivizing agriculture, and forcing peasants on to state-run collective farms, it had to eliminate the "kulaks," those prosperous peasants blocking the way to progress. In the Ukraine, this policy led to state-sponsored starvation for several million people. Religion and especially the Russian Orthodox Church had sanctioned and legitimized Tsarist authority with its superstition and elaborate rituals. Now this enemy of the people would give way to the new order through a combination of persecution on the one hand and the inculcation of state-sponsored atheism on the other. Because of Orthodoxy's deep roots in peasant society, collectivization and the war on the kulaks intertwined with the war on the church. New Atheist accounts dance around the issue by declaring Stalin's policies purely political in nature.

Marxism presented itself in the Soviet Union and elsewhere as the science that had unlocked the true direction of history. That lent an aura of infallibility to the Soviet Party as it carried out the dictates of Stalin and the leadership. What we now know as the infamous "Gulag" began as part of the economic planning for modernizing the Soviet Union. Those found guilty of opposing the state and party would pay with their labor, and the need for labor no doubt led to guilty verdicts to increase the numbers. Justification for these policies stemmed from Soviet ideology rooted in secular sources that cannot be credibly redefined by New Atheists as some sort of religion, political or otherwise.

Stalin also faced foreign enemies, especially among the powerful capitalist states in the West who had opposed the Bolshevik Revolution in its early years. In the early 1930s, he awoke only slowly to the Nazi threat, believing at first that Hitler's movement only signaled the imminent collapse of German capitalism. His attitude changed after 1936. In the Spanish Civil War (1936–39), he gave aid to the Loyalist forces against Franco's insurgent Nationalists, supported by Hitler and Mussolini. He then used the threat of "fascism" to purge the party, the bureaucracy, and the army in the Great Purge of 1936–38. The so-called show trials of 1937 and 1938 put his former Bolshevik comrades on stage for public confessions of spying for foreign powers, thus eliminating any possible challenge by them to his leadership. Even those who confessed their crimes in public court may have come to that through a deeply held belief that the Party could do no wrong, as Arthur Koestler sought to show in his novel *Darkness at Noon*.

By 1939, a revived and rearmed Germany had incorporated Austria into its borders and occupied first the Sudetenland and then the remainder of Czechoslovakia. Germany had signed an Anti-Comintern Pact with Italy and Japan aimed at stopping communism. It appeared that German Nazism and Soviet Communism faced each other as implacable ideological enemies. Then in August 1939, in a startling about-face, Stalin and Hitler struck a deal. Their two foreign ministers Molotov and Ribbentrop signed a nonaggression pact with a secret agreement to invade and partition Poland. On September 1, 1939, Germany struck across Poland's borders, followed 17 days later by a Soviet thrust into Poland from the east. Before the end of the month, Poland ceased to exist as an independent country.

The new partners seemed to vie with one another in a contest to eliminate Polish leadership. Intellectuals, government officials, and clergy became targets for both. In the most notorious incident, the Soviets executed 15,000 Polish officers in the Katyn forest and buried the bodies. After invading the USSR, the Germans exposed the atrocity and used it as prime propaganda to condemn Bolshevik barbarity. When the Soviets conquered the area later in the war, they went to elaborate lengths to manufacture evidence demonstrating that the Germans had done the deed. Following the collapse of the Berlin Wall in 1989, a newly independent Poland immediately launched an investigation into the Katyn massacre. The Russian government finally admitted the atrocity belonged to Stalin. In 2009, the leading members of the Polish government died as their plane crashed trying to land in stormy weather. They were on their way to a ceremony with Russian leaders at Katyn.

Stalin did put an end to persecution of the Orthodox Church during World War II as part of a campaign to rally national support against the German invaders. He summoned Russians to defend "Holy Mother Russia" rather than to defend the Bolshevik Revolution. Some Soviet citizens, especially non-Russians like the Ukrainians, initially welcomed the Germans as liberators. Others joined army units to fight with the Germans. Nazi mistreatment of their conquered subjects soon changed attitudes, and armed partisans harassed the German invaders. After the war, the Soviet Government continued a policy of limited cooperation with the Orthodox Church, only to reverse course under Khrushchev, who initiated a new round of antichurch policies in 1958.

Issues

This brief summary of Europe's history in the twentieth century incorporates two goals within the context of this book. First, it stays within the boundaries of what mainstream historians have written on the subject. It offers an introduction to twentieth-century Europe that sticks to commonly held views. Second, it covers ground also trod by our three New Atheist historians and their friends. In doing so, it reveals some important differences between these two versions of the recent past.

The main point in this chapter, and throughout the book, is that Dawkins, Harris, and Hitchens get history wrong. They marshal historical evidence to prove religion morally culpable of the greatest crimes of the past. In Europe, they target Christianity. Their arguments are often specious, nowhere more blatantly than in their treatment of twentieth-century Europe. Two characteristics stand out in their flawed history. Polemics constitutes the first. As in any debate, they want to score telling points against their opponents, and in history they believe they have a reservoir of damning evidence against religion. Ignorance constitutes the second characteristic. They present no evidence in their texts or notes that they have bothered to read much of what historians have written on the subjects they purport to cover. Many of their cited sources appeared decades ago, and they generally ignore the work of historians in recent decades or, even worse, sometimes misrepresent them.

Dawkins's apparent ignorance of the role of atheism in twentieth-century Marxism stands out as an example. When he claims, in reference to Stalin, there is "not the smallest evidence atheism systematically *influences* people to do bad things," he ignores massive evidence of a Soviet system of religious persecution that did many "bad things."[39] How is it possible not to know about these antireligious acts of the Soviet Union, from Lenin to Khrushchev, that historians have included in standard works on Soviet history? What sense does it make to declare that atheism is the "absence of belief" and therefore meant nothing in terms of a state policy that promoted atheism and attacked religion? Hitchens has his own version of a selective reading of the recent past. Why does he rely on one pioneering work on totalitarianism written six decades ago without bothering to sample the plentiful work since? Then there is the historical legerdemain of Harris. What is reasonable in his feeble attempt to make utopian secular ideologies look like religion? What all three seem adept at doing is changing the meaning of words to fit their polemics so that the word *religion* loses any meaning. Such manipulation of vocabulary has no place in historical discourse.

A subsequent book in support of the New Atheists came out in 2009: Victor J. Stenger's *The New Atheism*.[40] Stenger's earlier book *God: The Failed Hypothesis* makes the case for atheism based on his version of scientific reasoning. In this later effort, he perpetuates the flawed historical reasoning under review here, apparently believing that the version of twentieth-century Europe presented by Dawkins, Harris, and Hitchens needs defense rather than revision.

He takes on Stalin and his Soviet regime by first attacking professor and sociologist Paul Froese's *The Plot to Kill God* (2008), which chronicles and analyzes the effectiveness of the antireligious policies of the Soviet Union and its satellites. Stenger informs us of Froese's "claims that the Soviet Union waged a relentless war on religion that he attributed to the 'violence of atheism' and, despite this effort, it failed to eradicate faith."[41] Stenger gives no other information on the scope, evidence, and conclusions presented in Froese's book.

Froese presented well-documented evidence of the savage campaign against religious believers in the 1930s. Not surprisingly, he finds that the terror tactics of the regime and the relentless work of the League of Militant Godless led to a sharp decline in attendance at church services. The number of churches declined from 54,000 in 1914 to a low of 4,200 in 1941, rebounding during the war years to 16,000. Increased, if less savage, persecution in the Khrushchev and Brezhnev years resulted in 7,500 churches left open in 1966.[42] These and other statistics presented by Froese go unchallenged by Stenger, offering another instance of the New Atheists' inability or unwillingness to confront evidence out of step with their version of history.

Instead, Stenger goes on the offensive: "It turns out there is another side to the story, supported by hard evidence that disputes Froese's conclusion. In fact, since 1943 the Soviet Union has supported the Russian Orthodox Church. Despite that support, only 25 percent of Russians today are believers."[43] Only later does he mention but not explain or explore the context for Stalin's change in policy toward the church: World War II.[44] In the face of the rapid German advances after the invasion of the Soviet Union on June 22, 1941, the capture of several million Soviet soldiers, and the welcome the Germans received from some Soviet citizens as liberators, Stalin dropped references to Soviet Marxist orthodoxy in favor of traditional Russian patriotism to defend "Holy Mother Russia," including changing policy toward the Russian Church to garner popular support for the war effort.

The "hard evidence" he cites comes from two books. The first is *Stalin* by the writer and playwright Edvard Radzinsky, which appeared in 1997. Stenger reports facts from the book about priests being allowed to visit Soviet camps during the war, a religious procession in besieged Leningrad in 1943, and the election of a patriarch of the Russian Orthodox Church "with Stalin's permission."[45]

Stenger, in company with the New Atheists he praises in his book, presents facts out of context that ignore any understanding or account of Stalin's religious policies throughout the years of his rule. Indeed, he combines an omission of the persecution of churches and believers before World War II with a misleading suggestion that Stalin and the Soviet Union supported the church consistently during the war and after. Such an account of Soviet religious policy does not find a place in mainstream historical accounts for the simple reason that it is not true.

Moreover, Stenger misrepresents Radzinsky by neglecting the context given in the book. Radzinsky summarizes the early years of Soviet rule,[46] pointing out, "From the very beginning of the Bolshevik regime religion had been under attack . . . And Stalin was physically destroying church buildings, as Lenin had willed." Within a few years, although "80 percent of village churches were closed, people still enthused over the handful of churches reopened on Stalin's orders. He was skillfully reinventing a figure beloved of Russians: that of the good tsar with bad ministers."[47] Before the outbreak of the war, Stalin "had proclaimed a 'Godless Five-Year Plan' by the end of which (1943) the last church was to be closed and the last priest destroyed." The war changed all that for the moment, as Stalin began "his remarkable, and short-lived return to God."[48] Radzinsky points out that after the war Stalin put the church under the supervision of the NKVD (the Soviet secret police).[49] Thus Stenger distorts what Radzinsky had written about Stalin's policy toward religion and the Russian Orthodox Church.

The second book Stenger cites regarding Stalin's religious policies is *Fighting Words* (2005) by Hector Avalos. Avalos teaches religion and religious studies at Iowa State University. He shares both Stenger's atheism and his views on Soviet history. He "cannot find any direct evidence that Stalin's own personal agenda killed because of atheism," although he also states that "the idea that atheism was responsible for the mass terror under Stalin is partly true. Atheism was certainly a part of the reason for antireligious violence throughout the Soviet era. The larger factor, however, seems to be political." He does admit that church–state relations under Stalin "show both an atheistic reign of terror against religion, and a more conciliatory stance when it served Stalin's political purposes. Rather than representing some radical atheistic innovation, Stalin's normalization was more akin to the church-state unions common in many Western Christian countries."[50]

Avalos struggles, as Stenger and Dawkins do not, to give some context to Stalin's policies, but he gets muddled in trying to explain the relationship of religious, political, and economic factors during Stalin's regime. His most specific evidence consists of statistics about church life in 1944 when he cites large numbers of baptisms, attendance at Easter services in Moscow, and financial support Stalin gave to the church.[51] He makes no mention of World War II and the reasons Stalin temporarily reversed his attack on the church. Stenger seizes the statistics in Avalos's book, reproducing them in his as apparently the "hard evidence" he promised his readers.[52] Stenger and Avalos lecture us on Stalin's religious turnaround without taking into account the reason for it. Omitting something as obvious as World War II and its significance for this subject hardly inspires confidence in their ability to read historical evidence and put events into context.

Avalos and Stenger, in company with Harris, Dawkins, and Hitchens, avoid mentioning any of the ample evidence that might question the wisdom of their pronouncements about Stalin's religious policies. History texts on the Soviet Union under Stalin report repression of religion as an integral part of the stated goal of the Bolshevik regime to eradicate religion as a relic of the past. Bruce Pauley, in his study of totalitarianism in the twentieth century, comments, "The passive resistance of the Russian Orthodox Church against the antireligious policies of the state resulted in the confiscation of its property and long prison sentences and the execution of 8,100 Orthodox priests, monks, and nuns in 1922 alone. Hundreds of churches were destroyed in the 1920s and 1930s, including cultural monuments, for their building materials."[53] Robert Service's biography of Stalin informs us that "attacks on religious leaders became so frequent and systematic that the League of the Militant Godless expected belief in deities to be eradicated within a few years. Persecution was extreme, and only a twelfth of the Russian Orthodox Church's priests were left functioning in their parishes by 1941."[54] As another historian notes, the first objective of Soviet religious policy "was to annihilate religion by implementing severe legal restrictions on religious activity," and, she adds, an "anti-religious campaign, which varied in intensity, was sustained throughout the Soviet period."[55] If Avalos wishes us to believe that such atrocities were "more akin to the church-state unions common in many Western Christian countries," he might at least give us some examples of what he has in mind as evidence—perhaps the Church of England, or the Lutheran Church of Sweden, or maybe the French Catholic Church before its separation from the state in 1905? He doesn't tell us.

I have already mentioned Anne Nicol Gaylor and her atheist Freedom From Religion Foundation as a source for Dawkins's portrayal of Hitler. Gaylor also furnishes the following example of a historical understanding of Stalin's atrocities. She spoke on the subject in a debate with Fr. Leo Lefebvre, Professor of Theology at Georgetown University. When Fr. Lefebvre brought up Stalin and his death-dealing policies, she quickly asserted the New Atheist two-pronged assertion that religion causes war and death while atheism does not—then follows her sweeping and unsubstantiated generalization that "it certainly is true that more people have been killed in the name of God, than any other reason." As for Stalin, "he was seminary educated, and he was not killing in the name of atheism." Historians commonly mention Stalin's seminary training and its possible implications, but they never leave it there. It begins, rather than ends, the story of his beliefs and ideology. Gaylor favors a method of historical analysis that limits the discussion to comparing religion to atheism in order to condemn religion and exonerate atheism.[56] This myopic view of the past leaves out all other factors and circumstances. In this case, Gaylor omits any reference to Marxist ideology as relevant to the story of Stalin and the Soviet Union.

Avalos may be treading on unfamiliar historical ground in dealing with Stalin's policies. He mentions, for example, the so-called Living Church, also known as the Renovationist Church,[57] a reform movement attempting to combine Bolshevism with the Orthodox tradition and supported by the Soviet regime. Not surprisingly, the Russian Orthodox Church condemned the effort as "schismatic," especially, Avalos adds, "as it allowed married clergy."[58] His statement implies that the major issue dividing the Living Church from the Russian church was allowing a hitherto celibate clergy to marry. Historically the Eastern Orthodox tradition has always allowed married clergy, but it chooses its bishops from among the celibate monastic clergy. The Living Church wanted to allow married bishops and relax other rules pertaining to marriage of clergy, but that hardly constituted the main reason for the split. Avalos obscures the fact that Stalin's regime executed thousands of parish clergy, and not infrequently their wives, leaving many offspring of the clergy orphans.[59] The Living Church failed and went out of business by 1934 because of "traditionalism among the laity and also parishioners' recognition of the regime's attempt to bastardise (sic) Orthodoxy for political purposes."[60]

Stenger and Avalos illustrate one of the New Atheist methods of doing history: Ignore evidence contrary to your point of view and go searching for evidence that supports it. Recall that Stenger dismissed Paul Froese's book, *The Plot to Kill God*, without telling us anything about it. The book includes and assumes the kind of information we have just recounted about the systematic persecution of religion during the Soviet period that is consistent with what historians have known for decades. Froese's book differs not in substance, but in method, by using the tools of sociology to look at how religious institutions, belief, and practice survived over time under Soviet rule. His book contains many charts and graphs and a plentitude of data in standard sociological fashion. He wanted to find out to what degree religion survived in various locations in the Soviet Union and to what degree atheism had taken hold in the population. Reviewers have the job of assessing the evidence he presents and the conclusions he draws, but they recognize a serious scholarly piece of work. Stenger, for no reason he bothers to give us, just dismisses it and goes on to "hard evidence" that turns out to be extremely soft.

Stenger and Avalos also treat Hitler and the Holocaust in a manner consistent with the New Atheists. They play an either/or game that the evils of Nazism belong either to atheism or to religion, without entertaining any other categories of analysis. Since Hitler had Catholic roots and believed himself an agent of Providence, his crimes cannot be blamed on atheism. Historians would agree, and in fact, mainstream historians do not portray Hitler as an atheist, but they do also expend considerable effort on trying to explain and to understand Hitler's ideology with its core of biological racialism. For Stenger, the crimes of Hitler's regime "can hardly be assigned to the atheist side of the balance sheet." Therefore it can be assigned to the only other category on his balance sheet, religion: "So chalk up at least six million twentieth-century deaths to religion."[61]

The balance-sheet approach to history works for Avalos as well, who writes, "We will argue that the Holocaust neither was primarily grounded in atheism nor used atheism for its justification. In fact, we shall argue that the Holocaust has its roots in the biblical traditions that advocate genocide."[62] He thus asserts the Bible as the source of Nazi racial ideology without a mention of modern eugenics, Social Darwinism, and theories of racial hygiene that in fact informed Hitler and his henchmen.[63] Avalos's pronouncement fits well with Harris's assertion that the Nazis, in carrying out the Holocaust, acted as "agents of religion."

Mainstream historians strive to give a comprehensive account of what drove the Nazis to mass killing in the name of racial science. Fully aware of the role of traditional Christian anti-Semitism in the Holocaust, they also include the evidence of the role played by eugenics. As Richard Evans in *The Third Reich in Power* states, "Eugenics, including forced sterilization, was itself commonly accepted by scientists and commentators across the world as the modern face of social policy. For those who espoused it, belief in the centrality of race in human affairs also derived its legitimacy from what they regarded as the latest discovery of modern science."[64]

Hitler derived his moral universe from his preoccupation with advancing the Aryan race in keeping with what he believed constituted the laws of nature. Richard Weikart in his book *From Darwin to Hitler* concluded, "Hitler derided any morality inimical to the increased vitality of the 'Aryan' race, especially traditional Christian values of humility, pity, and sympathy. He considered those unnatural, contrary to reason, and thus detrimental and destructive for the healthy progress of the human species. He spurned the idea of human rights, calling it a product of weaklings."[65] Again, mainstream historians examine, discuss, and debate the roles of Social Darwinism and eugenics in the Holocaust, but unlike the New Atheists, they do not ignore them.

In another version of his binary argument on Hitler and the Holocaust,[66] Avalos gives us an example of a disturbing shortcoming of New Atheist historians: misrepresenting a source. He comments in passing, "Most of Stalinist violence resulted from forced collectivization, and recently published documents show the complicity of church authorities in the Stalinist agenda." His footnote cites only one book: Tatiana A. Chumachenko, *Church and State in Soviet Russia: Russian Orthodoxy from World War II to the Khrushchev Years* (2002). The book covers the period from 1943 to 1961. It deals with the rapprochement of church and state initiated by Stalin during World War II and then the turn back toward state repression of the church in the 1950s.

One review stated that "Chumachenko's work, however, shows that for the Russian Orthodox Church, de-Stalinization was a change for the worse. The increasing hostility toward the church during the 1950s reminded the Patriarch and the believers of the 1930s. The Khrushchev post-1945 generation took the freedoms of the church acquired since 1943 as counter-revolutionary and anti-Marxist, and thus decided to restrict and eventually eradicate the work of the church."[67] Chumachenko chronicles the implementation of a new campaign of repression against the Orthodox Church that took off in 1960, "an onslaught against church, believers, and clergy [that] acquired the character of a political war." She makes it clear that her book examines the process of change in the Soviet state's relationship with the church—"from toleration and peaceful coexistence to political struggle under slogans for the atheistic education of the population."[68] Avalos is simply wrong in stating that her book is about "the complicity of church authorities in the Stalinist agenda."

Historians know that our craft requires asking the right questions if we want to gain an understanding of the past. Asking whether atheism caused the Holocaust is the wrong question. The better question asks, What set of beliefs informed and motivated Hitler and Nazism? Historians have worked on that one for years. Recently Richard Evans devoted a one-hundred-page chapter to this subject in the second volume of his study of Nazi Germany.[69] Suffice it to say, Evans's detailed and nuanced presentation stands at odds with the misleading simplifications of the New Atheists. He deals, for example, with Nazism's goal of ultimately eliminating the Christian churches as beyond the regime's control and incompatible with its very nature. Evans also discusses the "political religion" metaphor as useful up to a point but misleading in that Hitler explicitly stated that his movement was not religious but secular: "A conceptualization of Nazism as a political religion, finally, is not only purely descriptive but also too sweeping to be of much help; it tells us very little about how Nazism worked, or what the nature of its appeal was to different groups in German society."[70]

Not surprisingly, Stenger and Avalos present history consistent with the views of Harris, Dawkins, and Hitchens. Stenger, in particular, wrote his book in defense and celebration of the New Atheists. Not only does he not question their version of the twentieth century; he accepts it and adds to it. A major concern of this book is that this kind of bogus history will replicate itself and become its own historiographical tradition, apart from mainstream history. I will return to this and other major issues in the final chapters.

The New Atheist version of the twentieth century betrays a number of historical errors of fact and method. One example is a lack of sufficient context to understand particular events and developments. Their method involves picking bits and pieces of the past that form no sequence or coherent pattern to help us understand those particular bits and pieces. The authors select whatever they believe will support their conclusions about the evil perpetrated by religion in history. Facts, as historians well know, do not speak for themselves. The historian's task involves reading and appraising evidence that they then put into historical context to bring coherence and understanding to the past. To select bits and pieces of information for polemical purposes to support a predetermined position falls outside the boundaries of accepted historical method. Historians try the difficult business of having the evidence drive them to conclusions rather than the other way around.

Another example of the flawed New Atheist method is that it points repeatedly to one cause when explaining events. Historical method, as it has developed since the Enlightenment, eschews such monocausal explanations. When historians attempt to understand the complexities of the past, they untangle many factors, forces, and motivations in reconstructing a plausible explanation for events. Understanding the reasons for world wars, totalitarian regimes, and the horrors of the past century means investigating a myriad of possible causes. To focus on one piece of the puzzle, such as religion, and argue that it takes precedence over all others makes nonsense of history. The result is an incomplete rendering of the past. Some historians label this practice "tunnel vision," which fixes on one factor to the exclusion of all else. To put it yet another way, it is history with blinders on that restricts a wider and more complete view of the past.

The New Atheists use history to support their point of view, but they show no interest in the discipline of history—namely, the search to understand the past according to the methods developed by historians in the past two hundred years. They dip into history as a polemical exercise selecting, not always accurately, material to fashion into weapons for their attack on religion and to demonize believers. They do not heed the good advice of historians about the craft of history. John Tosh, in his illuminating book *The Pursuit of History*, advises us that "almost any [historical] theory can be 'proved' by marshalling an impressive collection of individual instances to fit the desired pattern."[71] Dawkins, Harris, and Hitchens have the desired pattern, marshalling and manufacturing whatever historical evidence they can find to fit it. Intentionally or not, they and their allies deny the past by contorting it for the sole purpose of discrediting religion. They sacrifice any commitment to discovering historical truth to their unrelenting ideological preoccupation with demonizing religion. New Atheists believe that "religion poisons everything," and they find history useful only insofar as it supports this view.

Timothy Snyder makes an eloquent plea for the historian's obligation to understand even those who commit unspeakable crimes in his recent book, *Bloodlands: Europe between Hitler and Stalin*, a study of horrendous Soviet and German policies that killed 14 million civilians in eastern Poland, Belarus, and the Ukraine between 1933 and 1945. He acknowledges that we normally identify with the victims of these atrocities and condemn the perpetrators. Nevertheless, "it is less appealing, but morally more urgent, to understand the actions of the perpetrators. The moral danger, after all, is never that one might become a victim but that one might be a perpetrator or a bystander. It is tempting to say that a Nazi murderer is beyond the pale of understanding . . . To yield to this temptation, to find other people to be inhuman, is to take a step toward, not away from, the Nazi position. To find other people incomprehensible is to abandon the search for understanding, and thus to abandon history."[72]

The historical sensitivity that Snyder calls for is utterly lacking in the New Atheists.

CHAPTER 2

Europe from 1600 to 1900

> Above all, we are in need of a renewed Enlightenment, which will base itself on the proposition that the proper study of mankind is man, and woman.
> —Christopher Hitchens[1]

On November 10, 1793, the gothic Cathedral of Notre Dame in Paris assumed a new, modern identity as the revolutionary Temple of Reason to inaugurate the official Festival of Reason. Superimposed on the Christian altar was a new altar dedicated to liberty and inscribed "To Philosophy." A choir of young girls clad in white sang hymns to Reason. The flames flickered from the torch of Truth. At the end of the ceremonies the Goddess of Reason, portrayed by a local actress, made her appearance. Similar ceremonies took place in churches throughout the areas controlled by the revolutionary government.

This new state religion did not last. It came amid the Terror, the threat of foreign invasion, and the political emergence of Maximilien Robespierre as the radical leader of the revolutionary government. Robespierre executed his major rivals, including the leaders of the Cult of Reason, as he consolidated his control in early 1794. He then abolished the new religion, which he considered atheistic, and sought to replace it with his own version of a deistic state religion. On June 8, 1794, he established the Festival of the Supreme

Being. His motives may well have included both the political and the religious. According to one historian, "It is perfectly possible at one and the same time to see the Festival of the Supreme Being as a political maneuver and as a serious belief, the latter justifying the former."[2] Both of the revolutionary cults bore witness to the revolutionaries' attempts to replace Christianity with a proper civic religion to support the new order.

Robespierre himself fell to the guillotine later that year, and then the Terror abated. The revolution took a more conservative turn that culminated within a few years in the dictatorship of General Napoleon Bonaparte. As France's new emperor, he would abolish the revolutionary cults and forge a new alliance with the Church on his own terms. The cults of the French Revolution had tried but failed to translate the ideas of the Enlightenment into a new civic religion in place of Christianity. What Napoleon and the earlier leaders agreed on was the importance of state control over the church.

The vision of replacing or obliterating Christianity through fidelity to Reason, as exemplified by the Enlightenment, continues to appeal to those today who reject traditional religion. It is not surprising then to read Hitchens's vigorous call for "a renewed Enlightenment." In his version, the new Enlightenment will not depend "on the heroic breakthrough of a few gifted and exceptionally courageous people" as did the original. Now the study of literature and poetry will illuminate "eternal ethical questions" instead of relying on sacred texts that we now know to be "corrupt and confected." Unfettered scientific inquiry, with the aid of electronic means, will be open to masses of people. Sexual liberation from fear, disease, and tyranny will open new possibilities for a better world, provided "we banish all religions from the discourse. And all this and more is, for the first time in our history, within the reach if not the grasp of everyone."[3]

Hitchens concludes his book by rejecting any naïve, utopian dream of "progress" in a straight line. Progress will come not without struggle. "To clear the mind for this project, it has become necessary to know the enemy and to fight it." Throughout his book he has demonstrated conclusively that the enemy is religion. To forge a new world through Hitchens's "renewed Enlightenment," the forces of reason must do away with religion as the original Enlightenment failed to do. The new Enlightenment will triumph only when religion and religious believers disappear from the scene, and science and reason reign.

New Atheist History circa 1600 to circa 1900

Whether Hitchens's hope for the future is fulfilled remains to be seen. Our concern here rests with understanding the past, not with visions of the future. Hitchens, Dawkins, and Harris shape their historical arguments in conformity with the view that Europe in the seventeenth, eighteenth, and nineteenth centuries struggled to overcome wars over religion and then to embrace reason and enlightenment as paths to modernity. Their historical take on this period offers nothing new. In fact, they see the Europe from 1648 to 1914 in a traditional and, some would say, dated way.

The three authors adopt a view of European history popular in the Victorian era that posits a war between science and religion. This struggle had its origins in the triumph of Christianity that led to a dark age of a thousand years that we call the Middle Ages. Religious orthodoxy squelched wisdom and science as it ushered in centuries of superstition. Progress came to a halt. Only at the time of the Renaissance did a new day dawn that looked anew for inspiration to ancient Greece and Rome. The religious upheavals of the Reformation temporarily checked this renewal of civilization until the religious conflicts abated and secular authorities established sufficient stability, opening the way to the Enlightenment in the eighteenth century. Reason, science, and "positivism" took precedence over revelation, religion, and orthodoxy so that many Victorians looked forward to a future of continuous material and moral progress.

Dawkins, Hitchens, and Harris do not so much articulate this overarching historical narrative as assume it. Hitchens comes closest when he calls for a renewed Enlightenment. In his view, the eighteenth-century leaders of that intellectual awakening had broken the hold of Christian orthodoxy and opened the way for a more rational world. Now at the beginning of the twenty-first century we have the prospect of fulfilling Voltaire's wish to "crush the infamous thing" ("*Écrassez l'infâme*") of church and religion.

For Dawkins, moral progress comes with "the changing moral *Zeitgeist*" that makes our moral universe superior to those of the past. He, like Hitchens, acknowledges that moral progress does not develop in a straight line: "The advance is not a smooth incline but a meandering sawtooth." Nevertheless, he declares with great confidence that "most of us in the twenty-first century are bunched together and way ahead of our counterparts in the Middle Ages, or in the time of Abraham, or even as recently as the 1920s. The whole wave keeps moving, and even the vanguard of an earlier century (T.H. Huxley is the obvious example) would find itself way behind the laggers of a later century."[4]

Dawkins does not come up with a historical explanation for the causes that move forward the wave of moral advance—that push forward the moral *Zeitgeist*. Individual moral leaders certainly help: "We mustn't neglect the driving role of individual leaders who, ahead of their time, stand up and persuade the rest of us to move on." He cites the role of leaders in gaining racial equality and rights for women. He even acknowledges that some of this moral leadership had religious sources. He is careful to point out that while Martin Luther King Jr. professed Christianity, his nonviolent philosophy came from Gandhi. This qualification is his version of Hitchens's portrayal of King as in "no real as opposed to nominal sense" a Christian.[5]

Improved education also encourages us to understand that "each of us shares a common humanity with members of other races and with the other sex—both deeply unbiblical ideas that came from biological science, especially evolution." Then he brings in philosopher Peter Singer's views on moving to "a post-speciesist condition" that may be the wave of a future moral *Zeitgeist*. The important point for Dawkins is the ongoing moral progress as a fact of history for whatever reasons it happens: "The manifest phenomenon of *Zeitgeist* progression is more than enough to undermine the claim that we need God in order to be good, or to decide what is good."[6]

Harris subscribes to the Enlightenment narrative that casts religious teachings and practices into the past. His interpretation fits the ideas of nineteenth-century positivists like Comte, who believed that religion took precedence in the earliest stage of human development but that the dawning final and positive stage of the modern world would bring full human understanding of reality. Harris admits that religion gave meaning to life in the past, although that meant wars of conquest as well as notions of brotherly love. "But," he says, "in its effect upon the *modern* world—a world already united, at least potentially, by economic, environmental, political, and epidemiological necessity—religious ideology is dangerously retrograde."

Harris continues with the following remarkable passage, surveying the past with a laundry list of evils attributable to religion or, at the very least, religious-like postures:

> Our past is not sacred for being *past*, and there is much that is behind us that we are struggling to *keep* behind us, and to which, it is to be hoped, we could never return with a clear conscience: the divine right of kings, feudalism, the caste system, slavery, political duels, chastity belts, trial by ordeal, child labor, human and animal sacrifice, the stoning of heretics, cannibalism, sodomy laws, taboos against contraception, human radiation experiments—the list is nearly endless, and if it were extended indefinitely, the proportion of abuses for which religion could be found directly responsible is likely to remain undiminished. In fact, almost every indignity just mentioned can be

attributed to an insufficient taste for evidence, to an uncritical faith in one dogma or another. Religious faith represents so uncompromising a misuse of the power of our minds that it forms a kind of perverse, cultural singularity—a vanishing point beyond which rational discourse proves impossible. When foisted upon each generation anew, it renders us incapable of realizing just how much of our world has been unnecessarily ceded to a dark and barbarous past.[7]

Harris furnishes numerous examples taken from European history in the centuries prior to World War I so that we may distinguish between the good and the bad. Blaise Pascal from the seventeenth century and Søren Kierkegaard from the nineteenth century receive censure for coming up with new arguments for religious faith that Harris finds particularly offensive: "Pascal's wager, Kierkegaard's leap of faith, and other epistemological ponzi schemes won't do."[8] Pascal in particular should have known better. He was after all a mathematical prodigy, philosopher, and physicist who ended up wasting his final years dwelling on Christ's prophecies as proof of Christian truth.[9] Pascal may have had an intense conversion experience in 1654, but such experiences are not the exclusive property of Christians: "Hindus, Buddhists, Muslims, Jews, along with animists of every description have had these experiences throughout history. Pascal, being highly intelligent and greatly learned, should have known this; that he did not (or chose to disregard it) testifies to the stultifying effect of orthodoxy."[10] Dawkins also heaps scorn on Pascal's wager.[11] Hitchens characterizes Pascal's theology as "not far short of sordid."[12] The attack on Pascal by all three authors illustrates their penchant for issuing moralizing judgments on figures from the past rather than offering reasonable appraisals of the historical significance of such persons.

Harris asserts that we must not rely on the Bible, for to do so "is to repudiate two thousand years of civilizing insights that the human mind has only just begun to inscribe upon itself through secular politics and scientific culture." Those obstructing secular and scientific civilizing progress include not only religious extremists but religious moderates as well. In fact, the latter "are, in large part, responsible for the religious conflict in our world because their beliefs provide the context in which scriptural literalism and religious violence can never be adequately opposed."[13] In the historical world of Harris, moral progress is a fact and moderate religion a sham and a shame.

In the ongoing struggle between science and religion, Harris glimpses some hope that bad ideas "cannot survive the company of good ones forever." For example, "we are no longer killing people for heresy in the West." To make continued moral progress, we must "no more tolerate a diversity of religious beliefs than a diversity of beliefs about epidemiology and basic hygiene." We do not tolerate beliefs that put our health in danger, so why should we tolerate religious error?[14] Then in an endnote, Harris gives the recent example of China's mishandling of the SARS outbreak. If such mishandling ever led to a catastrophic threat to the rest of us, "there is little doubt that we would ultimately quarantine, invade, or otherwise subjugate such a society."[15] How that point relates to the threat posed by religious moderates is not clear, although the tone sounds ominous!

In terms of Harris's belief in moral progress, he sees Europe from the seventeenth to the nineteenth centuries slowly but surely shedding the errors of the past. The persecution of witches, so prevalent in previous centuries, wanes and dies by the early eighteenth century. Only the advent of science could successfully undercut belief in witchcraft and its practices.[16] Pope Pius VII finally condemned the use of torture in 1816.[17] The Spanish Inquisition called it quits in 1839 and the last auto-da-fé took place in Mexico in 1850.[18] Harris quotes approvingly Will Durant on the lesson we should learn from these barbaric practices of the past: "Intolerance is the natural concomitant of strong faith; tolerance grows only when faith loses certainty; certainty is murderous."[19] Harris never pauses to consider his own vocabulary of absolute certainty and manifest intolerance of views to the contrary.

Happily, progress through science gathered momentum as the barbaric practices of the past waned. Charles Darwin set sail on the *Beagle* and Michael Faraday discovered the relationship between electricity and magnetism about the time that the curtain rang down on the Inquisition. In the previous century, Voltaire had fought against the torture of heretics in one of France's final cases against a French Huguenot.[20] David Hume, Immanuel Kant, and other philosophers revolutionized ideas concerning epistemology and ethics. Harris does sound a cautionary note about "ransacking the armory of philosophers past" on morality and ethics, before employing a heavy dose of common sense.[21]

Harris devotes a chapter to "A Science of Good and Evil," in which he shows his debt to the nineteenth century. He argues for an ethic based on a pragmatism that rationally assesses questions of happiness and suffering. This approach stems from the utilitarianism of Jeremy Bentham early in the century. He claims that our ethical institutions "have their roots in biology." He dismisses the idea that religion might be the source of our "deepest ethical intuitions" and, in fact, states that to believe so is "absurd." Invoking the problem of theodicy—how a good and all powerful God allows evil—he concludes that we must face the obvious: "Theology is now little more than a branch of human ignorance. Indeed, it is ignorance with wings."[22]

Otherwise Harris has not much to say about the nineteenth century. Nietzsche gets one mention in an endnote.[23] Marx never appears, and there is one passing reference to Freud.[24] Comte and the development of the social sciences find no place in the discussion. All Harris has to say is that the great strides in scientific knowledge spawned attempts to use science in the understanding of human nature and society; hence the appearance of the new disciplines of economics, sociology, anthropology, and psychology in the nineteenth century.

Dawkins pays more attention to the nineteenth century, although he, too, never mentions Nietzsche or Freud and alludes only once to Marx.[25] Nevertheless, he does not hesitate to offer some striking generalizations about the period: "The nineteenth century is the last time it was possible for an educated person to admit to believing in miracles like the virgin birth without embarrassment. When pressed, many educated Christians today are too loyal to deny the virgin birth and the resurrection. But it embarrasses them because their rational minds know it is absurd, so they would much rather not be asked. Hence, if somebody like me insists on asking the question, it is I who am accused of being 'nineteenth-century.' It is really quite funny, when you think about it."[26] Funny or not, the issue raised here pertains to a historical narrative of the warfare between science and religion that does come from the nineteenth century. That does not make it true or false in and of itself, but it does speak to Dawkins's apparent ignorance or lack of interest in more recent historical views, including those on the history of science.

Dawkins does have his nineteenth-century heroes, including T. H. Huxley and, of course, Darwin. His only quarrel with Huxley is his agnosticism and failure to push farther into atheism. For Dawkins, unlike Huxley, the "existence of God is a scientific hypothesis like any other."[27] His references to Darwin appear more frequently, for Dawkins stands on firm scientific ground when discussing matters of biology and evolution. As for Darwin's historical impact on religion, Dawkins rightly observes that it was profound. He acknowledges that some great scientists before and after Darwin adhered to Christianity, but the number diminished as we passed into the twentieth century.[28] Like Harris, Dawkins does not bother with the new social sciences of the century. His one mention of Comte labels him a "celebrated French philosopher."[29]

Hitchens evinces more interest in the period from the seventeenth to the nineteenth centuries. He makes a greater effort than the other two to build the historical case for a new Enlightenment based, at least in part, on the success of the original Enlightenment. He discovers with great interest "how many great minds thought alike, and intersected with each other" in the eighteenth century. Benjamin Franklin, Edward Gibbon, David Hume, Thomas Paine, and Thomas Jefferson constituted a formidable phalanx of rational thinkers who challenged, albeit often cautiously, the prevailing Christian orthodoxy. Reason rather than revelation unlocked the secrets of nature and mankind. From Spinoza to these and other Enlightenment figures, Hitchens can then trace a line to Darwin in the nineteenth century and Einstein in the twentieth.[30]

The achievement of the Americans in forging a new constitutional order comes in for particular praise. Jefferson, Paine, and Franklin might carefully avoid the charge of atheism, but they led the way to "the writing of a democratic and republican constitution that made no mention of god and that mentioned religion only when guaranteeing that it would always be separated from the state."[31] These great figures "died without any priest by their bedside" even though some, like Paine, had to contend with much pestering "in his last hours by religious hooligans who demanded that he accept Christ as his savior."[32]

Dawkins also points to America's founders, their religious views, and their making of a new nation with a constitution omitting any reference to God. He believes that these leaders "would have been atheists" in our day, but the central point rests on their secularism. The secular foundation of the republic has gained support even from staunch conservatives like Barry Goldwater, whom he quotes at length on the subject.[33] Understandably, Dawkins expresses great concern over the present-day religious right in America that seeks to refashion a version of history with America founded as a Christian nation. He remains oblivious to the fact that he shares with them their manipulation of history to support predetermined points of view.

For Dawkins, the paradox has been and remains that the United States, "founded in secularism, is now the most religiose

[sic] country in Christendom, while England, with an established church headed by its constitutional monarch, is among the least." Dawkins tries his hand at explaining historically how this paradox came about. Perhaps, as a colleague suggested to him, all these immigrants, uprooted from stability in Europe, grabbed onto a church "as a kind of kin substitute on alien soil." He also considers the hypothesis that religiosity flourishes in a secular environment "where religion has become free enterprise. Rival churches compete for congregations—not least for the fat tithes that they bring—and the competition is waged with all the aggressive hard-sell techniques of the market place."[34] He misses the point that all tithes, fat or thin, are voluntary. Dawkins's concern, as always, remains not with finding valid historical explanations but with the threat today of continued religious belief and practice. Thus he ends his discussion with a series of quotations from Franklin, Jefferson, James Madison, and John Adams on the past and current abuses of the Christian religion.[35]

Harris does not give his historical views on the constitution and the people responsible for it. He does devote considerable space to a discussion of the threat of today's religious conservatives to the separation of church and state.[36] Nevertheless, he drops a few tidbits along the way that furnish further clues to his historical thinking. Prohibition, as we all know, failed, precipitating "a terrible comedy of increased drinking, organized crime, and police corruption. What is not generally remembered is that Prohibition was an explicitly religious exercise, being the joint product of the Woman's Christian Temperance Union and the pious lobbying of certain Protestant missionary societies."[37] Harris, like Dawkins, sounds the alarm to awaken us to the threat from the religious right and the "medievalism" that prevails in today's United States government.[38]

Harris offers occasional historical evidence to show that we have reached a more advanced moral sensibility than in the past, even the recent past. He mentions the New York City draft riots of 1863, with the

> streets ruled by roving groups of thugs; blacks, where not owned outright by white slaveholders, were regularly lynched and burned. Is there any doubt that many New Yorkers of the nineteenth century were barbarians by our present standards? To say of another culture that it lags a hundred and fifty years behind our own in social development is a terrible criticism indeed, given how far we've come in that time. Now imagine the benighted Americans of 1863 coming to possess chemical, biological, and nuclear weapons. This is more or less the situation we confront in much of the developing world.

We have even progressed beyond more recent atrocities such as My Lai in 1968. The point of these attempts at historical and moral analysis is to show that "as a culture, we have clearly outgrown our tolerance for the deliberate torture and murder of innocents. We would do well to realize that much of the world has not."[39] Harris has in mind Islam. At the time he wrote these passages, we had yet to learn of the abuses of Abu Ghraib, although he does know enough about the horrors perpetrated in the twentieth century that might have given him pause before making such pronouncements on our moral progress.

Harris presents history in a scattershot rather than systematic fashion. Nevertheless, he reveals his reason for culling the history of Christianity, which is to show us some of the historical horrors that "logically and inevitably" arose out of Christian faith. The "catalog of horrors," including Auschwitz, the Cathar heresy, and the witch hunts, "could be elaborated upon indefinitely." He urges readers to "consult the literature on these subjects," confident that such study "will reveal that the history of Christianity is principally a story of mankind's misery and ignorance rather than of its requited love of God."[40] Despite Harris's plea, he presents little evidence that he has found the time and energy to "consult the literature on these subjects" and many others.

Harris's use of history fits well with the historical views of Dawkins and Hitchens, whose books followed his. Dawkins cites *End of Faith* favorably[41] as well as Harris's subsequent book *Letter to a Christian Nation*,[42] while Hitchens mentions Harris once.[43] They share contempt and horror for religion, to be sure, but for our purposes it is their shared approach to history that needs scrutiny. Their books read like legal briefs that introduce historical arguments to make the case. Their method would gain recognition from lawyers as examples of "law office history." This method of doing history entails a premeditated search for bits and pieces of the past that support the conclusion you already have in mind.[44] That method may work in some court rooms, but it raises obvious questions in the court of historical discourse.

History 101: New Atheist and Mainstream History

The New Atheists concentrate much of their attention on several significant topics within European history from 1600 to 1900, such as the Scientific Revolution of the seventeenth century, the Enlightenment of the eighteenth century, and the Age of Positivism in the nineteenth century. Beyond these they have little or nothing to say about the political and economic developments of the period that mainstream historians find central, particularly the development of the modern, sovereign secular state and its attempt to subordinate the church, Protestant or Catholic, to the interests of the state. A review of these topics will set the stage for demonstrating again how New Atheist history fails to meet the test of historical veracity.

A prominent date in many textbooks of European history is 1648. It marks the end of the period labeled "The Age of Religious Wars" or "The Reformation Era." It signals the emergence of the modern state, modern diplomacy, and the growing secularization of politics. The Christian churches still counted for much in society but now had to take subordinate positions to the states, whether Catholic or Protestant. For the New Atheists, the only theme worth remembering is that of "religious war." The interplay of religion, politics, economics, and culture fails to attract their interest. Dawkins has told us, after all, that religious wars really are about religion and that is all we need to know.

The Thirty Years War (1618–48) began with religious divisions as central causes, but by its conclusion, secular state interests dominated. The war was really many wars that went through stages. By the end, Catholic France allied with Protestant Sweden as the two powers fought their common enemy, the Catholic emperor of the religiously divided Holy Roman Empire. A similar shift took place between England and the United Netherlands. The Elizabethans had aided their Protestant Dutch brothers against Catholic Spain. Once the Dutch gained their independence, they went to war with the English over commerce in a series of Anglo-Dutch wars. Economic rivalry, competition for territory, and "interests of state," rather than religious differences, now made up sufficient reasons to go to war. The nation-state, not the church, called the shots.

The continent no longer strove to become a unitary civilization as "Christendom" and settled into a "Europe" made up of sovereign competing states under governments with growing bureaucracies and regular armed forces. Conflicts got settled through some combination of war and diplomacy. The church, Catholic and Protestant, took a subordinate position to the secular power. No one paid attention to Pope Innocent X's protests over the peace settlement at Westphalia in 1648. Internally, religion was called on to provide legitimacy, unity, and stability, as summarized by Louis XIV's declaration of "One King, One Law, One Faith." England, on the other hand, had to sacrifice religious unity to maintain stability by granting a measure of toleration to Protestant Dissenters outside the established Church of England after the so-called Glorious Revolution in 1688–89.

England and France became rivals both in Europe and in developing global empires to compete with a declining Spain. The slave trade became an integral part of the new global economic order. The France of Louis XIV (1648–1714) emerged as an "absolute monarchy," with Louis declaring that "I am the state" ("*L'État c'est moi*"). England (Great Britain after the Act of Union in 1707 merged the governments of England and Scotland) went the way of a constitutional monarchy in which the Crown had to govern with Parliament.

Germany and Italy did not exist as political entities until their respective unifications in the second half of the nineteenth century. The Peace of Westphalia left the Holy Roman Empire with territories and cities that enjoyed sovereignty and left the emperor with little authority outside his or her Austrian territories. In the eighteenth century, Prussia created a strong army sufficient to win enough territory to rival Austria. In Italy, the pope continued to rule the Papal States that blocked any move toward unifying the peninsula until the *Risorgimento* several centuries later.

The seventeenth and eighteenth centuries witnessed a series of wars among the major powers both on the continent of Europe and in the territories of their overseas empires. Religion no longer played a major role in initiating these conflicts. The English, the French, the Spanish, the Portuguese, and the Dutch had established colonies that gave birth to a global economy and global warfare. Each power sought advantages through military, diplomatic, and economic policies. Louis XIV's bid to expand France's territory in Europe ran into a coalition of states led by William of Orange, now William III of England (1689–1702), to prevent French hegemony and maintain a balance of power. The coalition achieved a measure of success by the end of the War of the Spanish Succession in 1713 that, among other things, prevented the uniting of the French and Spanish thrones. These nonreligious wars do not gain the attention of our New Atheist historians.

Britain also succeeded in defeating the French in North America. Victory in the Seven Years War (1756–63), known in American history as the French and Indian War, gave Britain France's colony of Canada. The colonists rejoiced in the ouster of the French but resisted British efforts after the war to share in the cost. The issues of taxation and representation led to a worsening of relations between the colonies and the Mother Country, armed conflict in 1775, and the Declaration of Independence in 1776. The Americans, with French help after 1777, managed to hang on and then best their British masters. The peace settlement signed in Paris in 1783 recognized the independence of the United States of America.

France assumed a central position in eighteenth-century cultural and intellectual life as home of the Enlightenment in the so-called Age of Reason, a product of the seventeenth-century Scientific Revolution. That revolution had begun with the mathematical argument of Copernicus in 1543 that the sun, not the earth, is the fixed center of our universe, and it culminated with the mechanical universe of Isaac Newton (1642–1727).

The great figures of this revolution—Copernicus, Galileo, Brahe, Bacon, Descartes, Newton, and so on—used the tools of mathematics, observation, and experimentation to uncover the workings of nature and the universe. These methods suggested a new understanding of the relationship between human reason and divine revelation. Christians had debated that relationship since their earliest days. Now Christianity faced a new challenge that exalted the role of reason at the expense of revelation in the quest for knowledge.

As Newton laid out the new world governed by nature's laws, another Englishman, John Locke (1632–1704), laid the groundwork for a new understanding of human nature, psychology, and politics. He argued for the reasonableness of Christianity and the need for toleration, although stopping short of tolerance for Roman Catholics and atheists. His political treatises justified the Glorious Revolution and presented new ideas on the relationship of government to the governed. The new world of Newton and Locke quickly spread to France and the continent.

Voltaire led the charge in disseminating the ideas coming out of England. He and a host of thinkers known as *philosophes* encouraged the use of reason in all aspects of life, from abstract thought to everyday technology. Denis Diderot edited the multivolume *Encyclopedia* as a kind of compendium of useful knowledge. The *philosophes* had a range of beliefs on religion, from belief in God and an afterlife to atheism, but they shared hostility toward the Catholic Church. When Voltaire coined the phrase "*Écrasez l'infâme*," the infamous thing he had in mind was the church. Deism emerged from this movement as the most prominent religious belief. It posited a God or Architect of the Universe who created and set in motion the mechanical Newtonian world. God acted like a celestial clockmaker who set the clock, the universe, ticking, but no longer intervened. The Christian universe of creation, fall, sin, grace, and redemption disappeared. Human nature either was inherently good or could become good through education in right belief and conduct according to the new psychology. John Locke likened the human mind to a blank slate, a *tabula rasa*, that could then be inscribed with the right teaching. For many Enlightenment thinkers of the eighteenth century, as for the New Atheists today, traditional religion, including Christianity, represented superstition that must now give way to reason.

The leaders of the newly independent United States of America came of age at the height of the Enlightenment. Raised in Christian churches, they adjusted traditional Christian belief to fit the new rationality. Washington, Adams, Jefferson, Madison, and the others sought a religion more ethical than theological. The rivalry of Christian denominations led most of the Founding Fathers to favor religious toleration. The Constitution made no reference to God and did not require a religious test for federal officials. The First Amendment precluded the establishment of a national church. The momentum for this separation of church and state came from an unlikely coalition of figures such as Madison and Jefferson with Protestants, especially Baptists, who vigorously opposed an established church. The New Atheists give deserved credit to Madison and Jefferson while ignoring the Baptists.

The American Revolution initiated what historian R. R. Palmer dubbed the "Age of Democratic Revolution."[45] At its center in Europe stood the French Revolution, which began as a reform movement in 1789 and soon led to the toppling of the French monarchy and the execution of Louis XVI in 1793. Faced with widening domestic rebellion and threats from foreign powers, the revolution turned more radical under Robespierre and the Terror.

An early goal of the revolution included reform of the French church. The Civil Constitution of the Clergy in 1790 turned the clergy into paid servants of the state while curbing the influence and power of the church by confiscating church lands and property. The clergy initially divided over these changes, with many of the lower or parish clergy supporting the reforms. As the revolution took more radical form, including direct attacks on the church and clergy, a Catholic reaction set in. The explicitly anti-Christian stance of the new regime by 1793 and its attempt to impose a new religion of the state through the Cult of Reason or the Cult of the Supreme Being encouraged more widespread resistance among both clergy and laity.

The dictatorship of Napoleon Bonaparte brought about a resolution of the political, constitutional, and religious issues dividing France, at least for the moment. He forced Pope Pius VI (1775–99) into exile south of Rome. The year after Pius died, Napoleon signed a concordat with the papacy to end for the moment the conflict between his government and the church. In the longer run, the division over issues central to the French Revolution would continue in France and in the rest of Europe throughout the nineteenth century. The Congress of Vienna in 1815 brought an end to Napoleon and his European conquests and ushered in an age of reaction resting on an alliance of throne and altar.

Established churches, Catholic and Protestant, commonly opposed radical change that might bring about disestablishment in the name of reform.

Change, nevertheless, took place during the nineteenth century. Industrialization led to widespread migration from rural areas to cities, where workers often experienced poor housing and oppressive working conditions. Moderate socialists sought to organize workers to gain improved conditions while radicals called for revolution. Nationalists countered by seeking to rally all ranks of society in the name of national unity and strength. Historians commonly designate the nineteenth century an "Age of Nationalism."

The new prestige of science in the study of nature encouraged the development of the social sciences, which employed scientific methods to study humankind itself. The nineteenth century gave birth to a gamut of disciplines such as economics, anthropology, sociology, political science, and psychology. Some historians joined in by asserting that the study of the past also was a "science, no more, no less." Auguste Comte (1798–1857), Karl Marx (1818–83), and Sigmund Freud (1856–1939) sought new ways of understanding the human condition that had wide influence.

These thinkers and their disciplines furnished new reasons for skepticism toward traditional religious beliefs. Religious life included both high rates of participation, especially among the middle classes, and growing disenchantment of urban workers and growing skepticism among intellectuals. Religion for some seemed out of date, a relic of humankind's past, while the gains of science and technology fueled notions of progress. Charles Darwin's (1809–82) theories of evolution gave a new basis for understanding the world at variance with Biblical accounts. Darwin struck a fatal blow at traditional Christian arguments for a world designed by a creator-god.

At the same time, however, the European domination of the globe allowed Christianity to spread throughout the world in an unprecedented burst of missionary energy. Back home, Protestants and Catholics faced challenges that put them on the defensive. Anticlerical currents in France and Italy called for curbing the power of the Catholic Church, including threats to confiscate church property and limit the church's role in education. When the new Kingdom of Italy took over Rome in 1870, Pope Pius IX (1846–78) refused to recognize the Italian state and declared himself a "prisoner in the Vatican." From his point of view, the modern world, modern politics, and modern intellectual and cultural movements assaulted the Catholic Church from all sides. His *Syllabus of Errors* in 1864 rejected a list of modern beliefs, the final one being the idea that the "Roman Pontiff can and ought to reconcile and adjust himself to progress, liberalism, and modern civilization." He followed up with the Vatican Council of 1869–70, which articulated papal infallibility in matters of faith and morals.

Protestant churches faced challenges raised by science and historical criticism of the Bible. The variety of Protestant churches meant a variety of responses that ranged from a rejection of modernism by American fundamentalists to seeking accommodation with science and modern cultures in such trends as the Broad Church movement in the Church of England. T. H. Huxley coined the term *agnosticism* and debated Bishop Wilberforce over evolution.

The wars in Europe between the Napoleonic Era and World War I (1815–1914) shed relatively little blood compared to America's civil conflict. Nevertheless, war brought about changes in the European power structure. Prussia bested Austria in the Six Weeks War of 1866 that set the stage for German unification as Prussia defeated France in 1870–71. The Kingdom of Piedmont also managed to win some wars with French assistance that led to the precipitous and unexpected unification of Italy in 1861, following Giuseppe Garibaldi and his band of a thousand volunteers' invasion of Sicily and defeat of the Bourbon monarchy of southern Italy. Now the Great Powers of Europe—Great Britain, France, Germany, Italy, Austria-Hungary, and Russia—dominated international politics and diplomacy.

At the dawn of the twentieth century, both Americans and Europeans could look to the future with confidence. Despite the stresses and strains of industrial society, both continents enjoyed immense wealth and power. The United States had endured a bitter and bloody civil war followed by tremendous economic growth and a flood of immigrants from Europe. America sought to stay out of European affairs while expanding its own sphere of influence in the Caribbean and the Pacific. The Monroe Doctrine warned the Europeans to stay out of the Americas. European states tried to maintain a balance of power through their alliances and to establish colonies, especially in Africa, through mutual consent. Science and technology promised improvements in living conditions, and a general sense of progress pervaded society. For the more optimistic members of society, moral progress inevitably accompanied the technological and scientific advances of Europe and America.

Issues

The New Atheist version of history from the seventeenth to the nineteenth centuries assumes an interpretation of the European past that had its origins in the Renaissance, gained momentum in the Enlightenment, and reached full fruition in the Victorian age. This now outdated interpretation viewed Christianity as overcoming and quashing ancient culture, plunging Europe into a "dark age" of a thousand years. Only in the Italian Renaissance did a rebirth of antiquity lead to the first steps toward a new dawn in arts and letters based on new inspiration from ancient Rome and Greece. By the eighteenth century, Enlightenment reason and science took hold at the expense of religion and superstition. This opened the way to progress in the future, in both material and moral life. This narrative framework constitutes an interpretation of European history that became popular in the nineteenth century.

Two books dramatically made the case for science superseding religion. John William Draper's *History of the Conflict between Religion and Science* (1874) and Andrew Dickson White's *History of the Warfare of Science and Theology* (1876) portrayed science struggling to free humanity from the shackles of religious thought and religious institutions. Although White cautioned against the idea that religion and science were enemies, his book along with Draper's gave exactly that impression. It fit nicely with a Darwinian notion of "survival of the fittest"; presumably in this case, science was the fittest. The powerful warfare metaphor of these books had a tremendous impact in the following decades and furnished the next generation of rationalist scientists and philosophers with weapons to assault religion. Their legacy lives on with the New Atheists.

Adam Frank offers a telling anecdote on the influence of this Victorian view in his book *The Constant Fire* (2009). At age 16, his grandfather gave him a copy of Bertrand Russell's *History of Western Philosophy*, published in 1945. Russell, a favorite among the New Atheists, in his assault on John Calvin repeats Calvin's famous dictum, "Who will venture to place the authority of Copernicus above that of the Holy Spirit?" The young Frank relished the quotation as exposing the "foolishness of a religion blinded, resisting the facts of nature" and went on in adult life to quote it to his students in introductory astronomy. Only later did he discover in reading philosopher and historian of science Thomas S. Kuhn's attempt to authenticate Calvin's words that Calvin never said them. Kuhn could not find them anywhere except in White's *History of the Warfare of Science with Theology*. Frank concludes, "In fact, a detailed review of Calvin's writing reveals that he never made any specific comments on Copernicus. Whatever Calvin's feelings were about the heliocentric model, this quote appears to be propaganda in a war that started long after his time."[46]

The New Atheists accept both the overall view of European history from antiquity through Dark Ages to Renaissance, with a final breakthrough to Enlightenment and modernity, and its corollary, the implacable hostility between science and reason, and religion and superstition. The New Atheists' major addition to this master narrative resides less in its substance and more in the tone of scorn and disdain with which they make their arguments.

Today the primary challenge to these views comes from the history of science itself. Historians of science no longer employ the warfare model of Draper, White, and the New Atheists. These historians do not minimize or overlook the tensions between theology and science, including the objections of Pius IX to multiple aspects of modernity in the period when Draper and White wrote their influential books. In fact, those books reflected tensions of the time that have long since passed. The fact that Harris, Dawkins, and Hitchens cling to a Victorian view of the history of science does not, of course, mean they are wrong for that reason. It does indicate once again their lack of interest in what mainstream historians of science have produced in recent decades, and what these recent studies have to say on the relationship and interplay of religion, culture, and science.

The New Atheist position has a stake in maintaining the state of war between science and religion. War breeds and justifies extreme positions and justifies the wholesale condemnation of the enemy. Therefore, in the New Atheists' view, Draper and White got it right, and no appeals for moderation will change the nature of the conflict. Victor Stenger in *The New Atheism* reaffirms the "ancient war between science and religion" chronicled in Draper's and White's books. He vigorously denounces the late Stephen Jay Gould for trying to separate religion and science. He rejects the Templeton Foundation's efforts to reconcile science and religion and dismisses attempts "to minimize and even eliminate" the conflict. He even expresses some suspicion of such books as *Science and Religion: Are They Compatible?*, edited by atheist writer and philosopher Paul Kurtz.[47] Better, no doubt, from his point of view to avoid any possibility of calling a truce in the war between science and religion.

A forum of historians of science convened to answer the question, "How do we account for the persistence of the science-and-religion-in-conflict trope in the light of scholarship that has all but demolished the notion of a fundamental antagonism between two monolithic forces: science and religion?" Professor William R. Shea, who holds the Galileo Chair at the University of Padua, commented that Draper and White acknowledge that historians must enter into the minds of those they study in order to appreciate the "ideas, ambitions, and prejudices of the past," but "what they failed to grasp is that this can only be achieved if the historian is critically aware of his own ideas, ambitions, and prejudices. Self-knowledge is difficult at all times, but Draper and White had swallowed whole a view that made it impossible for them to exercise self-criticism. They believed that the scientific method ushered in by the Scientific Revolution provided them with a way of understanding not only nature but history."[48]

Professor Michael Ruse, zoologist, philosopher, and atheist, also suggests that the war between science and religion no longer holds sway in studying intellectual history: "In fact, this 'warfare' metaphor, so beloved of nineteenth-century rationalists, has only a tenuous application to reality. For most of the history of Christianity, it was the Church that was the home of science." He goes on to comment that "the truth seems to be that much of the supposed controversy was a function of the imagination of non-believers (especially Thomas Henry Huxley and his friends), who were determined to slay theological dragons whether they existed or not."[49]

This book contends that the New Atheists, whatever their understanding of science, do not understand history and do not follow standard historical methods. They present historical subjects with great certitude without demonstrating any knowledge of the work of distinguished historians on those subjects. Their declarations and assertions on the history of science and religion in this period furnish a striking example. They present a world of black (religion) and white (science) with no shades of gray. Consequently they display none of the prudence and care with which historians approach and present complex historical subjects.

Steven Shapin in his book on *The Scientific Revolution* devotes twenty pages to the relationship of the new science and religion in the seventeenth century. He begins the discussion by cautioning against a modern impression of the opposition between science and religion: "It is time to systematically correct any such impression, for in the sense in which early modern changes in natural philosophy 'threatened' religion or were animated by irreligious impulses needs to be very carefully qualified or even denied."[50]

Another problem with the historical framework of the New Atheists stems from the assumption of moral progress, most notably in Richard Dawkins's talk of the changing and improving moral *"Zeitgeist."* We encounter again the Enlightenment idea that progress in science and technology, based on reason, led to moral progress as well. Harris's assertions on the subject also come through clearly enough, but he fails to offer any evidence for his confident assurances of the "civilizing insights" of the past two millennia and just how it came about that we occupy a moral position superior to that of the 1863 draft rioters in New York. Dawkins and Harris both may have a point that we have advanced over the centuries in our moral ideas and sensitivities. Nevertheless, they offer no specific historical reasons why and how the change came about, and they do not face up to the moral atrocities of our day.

Instead we get vague assurances that "the whole wave" of moral progress continues to carry us along.[51]

Historian John Lukacs warns against presenting ideas and beliefs as abstractions that are outcomes of "some kind of *Zeitgeist.*" He makes the point that individuals do not "*have* ideas. They choose them."[52] Historians constantly face the challenge of how, why, and when historical characters chose the ideas and beliefs that animated their actions. It does not suffice to make vague and abstract appeals to the *Zeitgeist*, what was "in the air," or to assume the inevitable triumph of one set of beliefs at the expense of another. In addition to these problems, the New Atheists have the daunting task of squaring the circle by showing that their brand of science and rationality leads to a morality and to moral progress.

Harris leads the pack in the effort to link science and morality. In his recent book, *The Moral Landscape*,[53] he argues that science can and should be the basis of morality. Although the book and its subject go beyond our historical considerations here, he makes the case for a morality based on a type of utilitarianism that originated in the early nineteenth century with Jeremy Bentham. In a review of the book, H. Allen Orr expresses skepticism of Harris's lack of historical and cultural perspective: "And Harris doesn't seem to take seriously the fact that different peoples at different times have had different visions of morality. When Trotsky said, 'We Bolsheviks do not accept the bourgeois theory of "the sanctity of human life,"' was he endorsing Harris's 'beneficence, trust, creativity,' and 'wholesome pleasures,' all enjoyed in a 'prosperous civil society?'"[54] Orr's critique fits with Lukacs's admonition that historians must deal with the particular circumstances of any moment in the past when examining ideas and beliefs, including those about morality.

While Harris delivers his own version of a new science of morality, Hitchens pins his hopes on a future new Enlightenment. Both keep up the barrage of historical examples taken out of context to buttress their case for a better future. Most of us agree no doubt with Harris that Prohibition failed and had negative side effects such as corruption of public officials, increased drinking, and the growth of organized crime. As we have seen, he blames religion in the guise of the Women's Christian Temperance Union. On the other hand, historians place the rise of the temperance movement within the context of a variety of factors, not the least of which was the high incidence of alcoholism that had ugly consequences for women and children. The historian's obligation to guide us in understanding the past means putting important events in some rational context. The New Atheist historians avoid such a practice for fear it would dull their assertion that religion remains the source of most or all or the worst evils of the world, but they remain oblivious to the fact that repeating assertions without offering evidence to support them does not equal credible history.

Novelist Marilynne Robinson rebuked Dawkins for "his consistent inattentiveness to history" and his inconsistency when dealing with his "selective reading of the past." Dawkins regretted that his favorite "enlightened and liberal progressive" T. H. Huxley had commented in 1871 that "no rational man, cognizant of the facts, believes that the average negro is the equal, still less the superior of the white man." Dawkins defends Huxley by noting that "it is commonplace that good historians don't judge statements from past times by the standards of their own."[55] His belief that the whole wave of the moral *Zeitgeist* keeps moving just confirms his view that even past progressives like Huxley would be the "laggers" of a later time.[56] In fact, as we shall see in repeated examples, the New Atheists commonly do "judge statements from past times by the standards of their own."[57]

The most glaring omission in the New Atheist account of Europe and America from 1600 to 1900 has to do with the rise of the modern, sovereign state and what that meant for the role of religious institutions in Western societies. Their resulting history concentrates on condemning religion for committing evil acts while exonerating atheism, all with the politics for the most part left out. Their method enhances their polemic against religion, but it diminishes their credibility as historians.

Political and other factors often joined religious divisions in armed conflicts. Even though the Thirty Years War commonly gets on the list of "religious wars" for obvious reasons, historians agree the conflict did not solely involve religion. As David Cannadine recently put it, "In his conduct of French foreign policy, Cardinal Richelieu held the view that 'the interests of state and the interests of religion are two entirely different things.'" For interests of state, Richelieu joined with Protestant powers to oppose the Catholic Habsburgs.[58] When Dawkins asserts, "Religious wars really are fought in the name of religion, and they have been horribly frequent in history," he gives no examples, and the only source he quotes is Sam Harris. Dawkins is on board with the binary view of history, religion versus atheism, so that atheism is absolved of causing wars: "Why would anyone go to war for the sake of an *absence* of belief?"[59] Dawkins appears highly motivated by his "absence of belief" in *The God Delusion*, while he is unable to understand how atheism has been part of ideologies that do, as a matter of fact, drive the agenda of political regimes. This point does not charge all atheists with starting wars or committing atrocities. It only upholds the role of atheism in modern intellectual, cultural, and political history.

Victor Stenger's summation of the New Atheism at the end of his book speaks approvingly of Harris, Dawkins, and Hitchens's version of history. Concluding his clumsy appraisal of Stalin's religious policies, Stenger makes this historical generalization: "One does not measure evil by the numbers killed. Is killing ten innocent people worse than killing one? Every king, pope, crusader, or inquisitor who unjustly killed a single person committed an evil act. And history records far more people killed in the name of religion than who did so in the name of unbelief."[60] This approach to history excludes consideration of other reasons for conflict and killing that might involve politics, economics, culture, and the myriad factors real historians grapple with in seeking an understanding of the past. Stenger remains mired in a view of the past distorted by his version of balance-sheet history, which arbitrarily and inappropriately puts "religion" on one side of the ledger and "unbelief" on the other. One will search in vain for such a balance sheet or ledger among mainstream historians. When Stenger confidently declares what "history records," he omits any reference to the historical record.

The modern state sought to subordinate religious institutions. Revolutionary France took a new path by abolishing the monarchy as it sought to reorganize and control the Roman Catholic Church without gaining papal approval. In its most radical phase, the Republic tried to substitute a state civil religion for Catholicism. When the peasants in the western region of the Vendée rose in protest for a number of religious, political, and economic reasons, including conscription in the army, they faced savage countermeasures by the state. The state massacred thousands of peasants in a savage civil war that pitted the Republican army against the peasants and the church. In one incident, a Republican leader "decided to economise [sic] on musket balls and powder" by drowning prisoners in the Loire. "Priests were prominent among the eighteen hundred victims of these 'noyades,' which were allegedly a humane response to epidemics and overcrowding" in prisons. "As a result of these atrocities, which involved such scenes as young women stretched upside down on trees and cut almost in half, up to a third of the population perished, a statistic roughly equivalent to the horrors of twentieth-century Cambodia."[61]

Violence in the name of the state became commonplace in the nineteenth and twentieth centuries, but the New Atheists ignore that piece of modern history lest it diminish their insistence that religion, and religion alone, is responsible for history's worst atrocities. Ideology trumps historical accuracy.

Following German unification in 1871, Bismarck sought to control the Catholic Church and its cultural and political influence in the so-called *Kulturkampf.* The Protestant majority sympathized with these anti-Catholic measures. The May Laws of 1873 imposed restrictions on the education of clergy and gave the state authority to veto church appointments. So heavy and clumsy were the state attempts to control the Catholic Church that even some Lutherans began to worry that they might be next. In addition, the state lacked the resources to implement fully its hold over the church. The struggle between the new German state and the Catholic Church found resolution through negotiations with the Vatican shortly after Leo XIII assumed the papal throne in 1878.[62]

These two well-known examples of church and state relations in modern Europe remind us that the religious and ecclesiastical history of Europe has more to it than the simplistic dichotomy between "religion" and "unbelief." In fact, the New Atheist treatment of history relishes sweeping generalizations with little or no support from specific evidence. They point the finger at religion as the major cause of evil and war throughout history. Neither the conquests of Louis XIV in the late seventeenth and early eighteenth century nor Napoleon's attempt to overrun the continent in the early nineteenth support such a view. And while our own bloody Civil War had its religious elements, it hardly qualifies as a "religious war." The New Atheist repetition of unsubstantiated generalizations does not make them true.

Mark Gilderhus, in his brief survey of Western historical thinking, *History and Historians,* comments on how complicated is the task of grasping truth about the past. He quotes the "observation by philosopher W. H. Walsh, that in truth 'history is an altogether stranger and more difficult discipline' than it is often taken to be."[63] Unfortunately, the New Atheists present history with no awareness of the challenges and difficulties in reconstructing the past and prefer instead to subordinate historical understanding to their own polemical purposes. Thus history as an autonomous discipline with its methods and rules of reasoning disappears. We are left only with simplistic versions of the past constructed for whatever political or ideological agendas we wish to pursue.

The New Atheists fabricate a vision of the past that lacks a rational approach to human history and do so in the name of reason and science. Much is at stake. If there are no boundaries to historical discourse, if anything goes so long as it fits one's political, religious, philosophical, or cultural stance, if, in fact, history contains no objectively verifiable truth, then we forfeit the possibility of illuminating the human condition through examining our past. That is the larger issue at stake in New Atheist historiography.

CHAPTER 3

Europe to 1600

> If God defines what is good and what is evil, then those who follow God's commands are morally justified to commit similar atrocities. History shows the results: holy wars, burning of heretics, the Crusades, the Inquisition, the Thirty Year's War, the English Civil War, witch hunts, cultural genocide, brutal conquests of the Aztecs, Incas, and Mayans, ethnic cleansing, slavery, colonialist tyranny, and pogroms against the Jews eventually leading to the Holocaust.
>
> —Victor Stenger[1]

On December 29, 1170, four knights confronted Archbishop Thomas Becket before the high altar of Canterbury Cathedral. They sought to cow Becket into submission to his former friend and confident King Henry II. They specifically demanded that he lift his excommunication and suspension of two bishops who had supported Henry in his quarrel with Becket. The archbishop, England's highest ranking cleric, refused. The enraged knights set upon him, intending to drag him from the church, but his resistance led to first one, then another, dealing him blows that proved fatal.

Soon the faithful attributed miracles to the martyred archbishop. Within three years, Pope Alexander III canonized him. In 1174, Henry II did penance at Becket's tomb and walked barefoot through the streets of Canterbury while enduring the flogging of monks. The cult of St. Thomas flourished in the coming centuries as pilgrims flocked to his shrine. When Henry VIII took on the papacy in the sixteenth century, he destroyed the shrine as he severed the English Church from all ties to the Bishop of Rome.

What had led Henry II to purportedly utter the now well-known question, "Who will rid me of this meddlesome priest?" The issues dividing the two concerned a deepening rift between the spiritual authority of the church and the temporal authority of the crown in England and throughout Europe. In this case, Henry and Thomas clashed over who had the authority to adjudicate clergy guilty of felony crimes such as rape and murder. When Henry extended royal jurisdiction to such cases in 1164, Becket's opposition led him to six years of exile in France. In 1170, the king and the prelate met in Normandy and reconciled, allowing the latter to return on November 30. Then his refusal to absolve the Bishops of London and Salisbury for their crime of backing the king led to the infamous murder in the cathedral a month later.

The roots of this dispute date from the previous century, when Pope Gregory VII planted the notion that the priestly authority of the pope came directly from God and therefore ruled over kings and even the Holy Roman Emperor. The papal position asserted that each realm of authority, spiritual and temporal, had its proper sphere, but when push came to shove the spiritual was superior, just as the light of the sun outshines that of the moon.

The radical reforms of Gregory VII sought to free the papacy of lay control and to subordinate all bishops and archbishops to popes, not kings. The reforms amounted to a revolution in the relationship of the ecclesiastical and royal authorities that set the stage for the tangled church–state relations of subsequent centuries, a major theme of European history in the Middle Ages and beyond. Readers will search in vain for any hint of this major subject in the New Atheists' abundant comments on Europe's history. The criticism here does not suggest they have any obligation to cover every facet of that history, but it does suggest that they should offer better evidence that they know what they are talking about in their frequent pronouncements on the past. The New Atheists lack a grasp of the larger historical context within which Europe developed, preferring to pick out the bits and pieces that fit their defined position.

The New Atheist Version of Europe to 1600

The New Atheists operate within a grand historical narrative that sees the rise of Christianity as a repudiation of the superior civilization of Greece and Rome. When the Roman Emperor Constantine embraced Christianity, he set in motion the transformation of a persecuted sect into an imperial institution. He used the church to legitimate his authority. His initiative brought about the Council of Nicaea in 325 to resolve doctrinal differences and enhance his own control of the church. Before the end of the fourth century, Christianity became the official religion of the empire, thus leading ultimately to the extinction of the traditional pagan cults.

According to the New Atheists, the Christian Roman Empire turned intolerant and close-minded. Greek rationality and Roman religious toleration fell as the church hammered out its orthodoxies and defined the heresies it would not countenance. The church championed celibacy as a superior way of life and took repressive attitudes toward sexual expression. These early developments cast a long shadow on the subsequent development of Europe that meant a period of darkness for centuries until a rediscovery of ancient civilization could set in motion the path to rationality, science, and modernity.

Not surprisingly, the New Atheists have little to say about the so-called Dark Ages from the late Roman Empire to the eleventh century. All historians recognize that the "darkness" comes in part from the relative paucity of sources for these centuries following the breakup of the Roman Empire and the early formation of a European as opposed to Mediterranean civilization and culture.

In addition, the New Atheists find the period worthless, a time of darkness thanks to the collapse of ancient civilization and the triumph of the religion and superstition of the Christian Church. Nothing of value appeared over the next millennium—the less said about it the better.

The notion of a "dark age" between the sunnier times of antiquity and the new dawn of the Renaissance became a fixed doctrine during the Enlightenment. Edward Gibbons's *Decline and Fall of the Roman Empire* put the finger on Christianity as guilty of undermining the vigorous civilization of Rome. The end of Rome and the triumph of Christianity meant the death of science and reason for at least a thousand years. Intellectual and moral progress could not take place in a society dominated by religion. Christopher Hitchens felt compelled to spell it out for us: "Religion comes from the period of prehistory where nobody . . . had the smallest idea of what was going on. It comes from bawling and the fearful infancy of our species, and is a babyish attempt to meet our inescapable demand for knowledge (as well as for comfort, reassurance, and other infantile needs)." After all, even the least educated of Hitchens's children knows "much more about the natural order than any of the founders of religion."[2]

Two popular books among the New Atheists help us to understand their views on the end of Rome and the formation of medieval Christian Europe. The first is Charles Freeman's *The Closing of the Western Mind: The Rise of Faith and the Fall of Reason*, cited in the bibliography of Dawkins's *The God Delusion*. Harris makes heavy use of the second: William Manchester's *A World Lit Only by Fire: The Medieval Mind and the Renaissance, Portrait of an Age*. Together they form a firm foundation for the New Atheist historiography of the Dark Ages.

Freeman's engagingly written book argues that the Greek intellectual tradition did not simply peter out: "Rather, in the fourth and fifth century A.D. it was destroyed by the political and religious forces which made up the highly authoritarian government of the late Roman empire."³ From St. Paul on, Christian leaders favored revelation over the reason and wisdom of Greece, effectively cutting off science until Aquinas opened the door again in the thirteenth century. Finally Copernicus in the sixteenth century "set in hand the renewal of the scientific tradition."⁴ Freeman assumes the metaphor of warfare, suggesting that Paul's condemnation of the philosophers (I Corinthians 1:19) "was the opening shot in the enduring war between Christianity and science."⁵ Paul's denunciation of Greek philosophy began to erect a barrier "between science—and rational thought in general—and religion that appears to be unique to Christianity." Thus Christianity "challenged a well-established and sophisticated tradition of scientific thinking."⁶

William Manchester gained his reputation as a writer for a variety of fiction and nonfiction books. In particular, he became nationally known for several of his biographical efforts: *Portrait of a President: John F. Kennedy in Profile* (1964) and *Death of a President* (1967); *American Caesar: Douglas MacArthur* (1978); and *The Last Lion: Winston Spencer Churchill* (1984–2012) in three volumes, the final one published eight years after Manchester's death. An illness interrupted work on that third volume of the Churchill biography. While convalescing, he decided to turn his attention to writing the introduction to a friend's forthcoming book on Ferdinand Magellan that, in turn, led to investigating the background and context for Magellan's circumnavigation of the globe in the sixteenth century. Instead of several pages as prelude to the great explorer, Manchester wrote a book that tried to paint a "portrait of an age" from the Middle Ages to the Renaissance: *A World Lit Only by Fire* (1992).

Although Manchester had some grounding in sixteenth-century history, he realized he needed a "fresh start" in grasping the period leading up to the changes of that century and Magellan's historic voyage.[7] First he had to determine what authorities to use in constructing his account. Three volumes from Will Durant's *Story of Civilization* topped his list of references: *The Age of Faith*, *The Renaissance*, and *The Reformation*. Durant's massive 12-volume effort gained a wide readership in the 1950s and became known to a whole generation of subscribers to the Book of the Month Club as a gift for joining. In addition, Manchester found *The New Cambridge Medieval History* "another towering monument of historicism" to guide him. Coming in third on his list, the *New Encyclopedia Britannica*, fifteenth edition, contained informative articles by world-class scholars. Beyond these he listed an impressive bibliography of secondary works running to seven pages.[8]

The "medieval mind," the subject of Manchester's opening chapter, did not amount to much thanks to the dreary conditions of the Dark Ages. Rome succumbed to countless barbarian incursions that broke up the civilized Roman world. On top of that catastrophe, famines and plagues further depleted the population and stifled spirits. The church converted the Germanic tribes, but Manchester understandably remains skeptical of how much Christian teaching penetrated the rank and file. No wonder then that medieval men, "crippled by ten centuries of immobility . . . viewed the world through distorted prisms peculiar to their age." He concludes that in all that time, Europe produced few inventions, no startling new ideas, and explored no new territories. For 1,436 years, Manchester intones, the successors of Saint Peter, "all chosen by God and all infallible," held sway over a society in which "all knowledge was already known. *And nothing would ever change.*"

Manchester's masterful pen goes on to set the stage for the "shattering" of this world that like a "mighty storm" would sweep over Europe: "Shackled in ignorance, disciplined by fear, and sheathed in superstition, [Europeans] trudged into the sixteenth century in the clumsy hunched, pigeon-toed gait of rickets victims, their vacant faces, pocked by smallpox, turned blindly toward the future they thought they knew—gullible, pitiful innocents who were about to be swept up in the most powerful, incomprehensible, irresistible vortex since Alaric has led his Visigoths and Huns across the Alps, fallen on Rome, and extinguished the lamps of learning a thousand years before."[9]

The New Atheists might take issue with the last sentence, since they are convinced that the Christian Church, rather than the Huns, "extinguished the lamps of learning." Although atheist philosopher Alex Rosenberg dismisses history, including the New Atheist master narrative, as useless in his recent book *The Atheist's Guide to Reality*, he credits Manchester with showing us that "there has been some progress in human history" since the Black Death.[10] As one reviewer of the book noted, "Scientism, whether Rosenberg's today or E. O. Wilson's a generation ago, is impatient with history. ('The Atheist's Guide' declares it to be 'bunk.')"[11]

The dreary centuries depicted by Manchester stem from the writing of St. Paul and the Emperor Constantine's support for the Christian Church, which together set the stage for the subsequent troubled and troublesome history of medieval Christianity. Paul put women in a subordinate position to men, put down sex while favoring chastity, and repudiated the philosophers. Constantine used the church for his own political purposes, which led to heresy hunting and Christian anti-Semitism. When Christianity became the official religion of the Roman Empire later in the fourth century, the imperial church imposed orthodoxy on the population, setting out on a path that would led to the Crusades and other bloody means to spread and enforce the faith.

Will Durant, Manchester's major source, subscribed to the master narrative vigorously presented by Manchester and common to New Atheist history. Durant, nevertheless, had more good to say about the medieval legacy than either. He acknowledged advances in literature, art, politics, religion, economics, and education.

He found, for example, that "the intellectual legacy of the Middle Ages is poorer than our Hellenic inheritance, and is alloyed with a thousand occult perversions mostly stemming from antiquity. Even so it includes the modern languages, the universities, and the terminology of philosophy and science." Although the scientific legacy was more modest, it "includes the Hindu numerals, the decimal system, the conception of experimental science, substantial contributions to mathematics, geography, astronomy, and optics, the discovery of gunpowder, the invention of eyeglasses, the mariner's compass, the pendulum clock, and—apparently the most indispensable of all—the distillation of alcohol."[12] Despite his own biases, Durant immersed himself in history and displayed lots of good historical sense in his voluminous study.

Manchester would have done well to pay more attention to Durant and, beyond him, to historians of medieval Europe. Medieval scholar Jeremy du Quesnay Adams began his review of *A World Lit Only by Fire* in the journal *Speculum* by calling it "an infuriating book." He went on to remark that the book contained "some of the most gratuitous errors of fact and eccentricities of judgment this reviewer has read (or heard) in some time."[13] *Kirkus Reviews* found the book "a disappointing retread of past histories about the explosive dawn of the modern age. For Manchester, the Middle Ages were a period of unrelieved superstition, corruption, violence, anti-intellectualism, and intolerance." Manchester admitted he had not bothered with recent scholarship. His treatment of his subject "has lost all nuance," simply "picturing the Middle Ages . . . as altogether bad."[14] For the New Atheists, the weaknesses pointed out by professional historians become strengths in making their case against medieval Europe.

The New Atheists agree with historians in general that St. Augustine of Hippo laid the intellectual foundation of medieval Europe, but they do not conceal their dislike for him and his legacy. His teaching on original sin led to the "unhealthy preoccupation of early Christian theologians with sin" that has marred Christianity ever since.[15] Augustine believed that error has no rights with truth, thus sanctioning the use of force against heretics.[16] In spite of, or maybe in reaction to, his own sexually promiscuous early life, he reinforced Christianity's tendency to repress sexuality and to identify sex with sin.

The New Atheists have no reason to examine the Dark Ages that followed Constantine, Augustine, and the fall of the Roman Empire. Their interest in the medieval period focuses on the negative effects of Christian domination of Europe revealed in the Crusades, the Inquisition, witch hunts, and other means of imposing orthodoxy. For them, the root problem lay in an irrational faith that sought to bring all Europeans within the fold of the church.

Harris devotes more time and effort to spelling out the problematic character of medieval Christian society with its "theocratic terrors"[17] than his fellows. He follows the development of the Inquisition from its twelfth-century beginnings to its bitter end centuries later. Originally the Inquisitors went after the popular but heretical sect of the Cathars, also known as Albigensians, who had particular strength in southern France. Innocent III at the Fourth Lateran Council in 1215 recognized the Dominican Order whose members became the chief enforcers for the Inquisition. When Innocent decreed that the property of convicted heretics would go to the church, it only gave added incentive to hunt down the unorthodox.[18] Harris maintains that faith itself explains how the church "managed to transform Jesus' principal message of loving one's neighbor and turning the other cheek into a doctrine of murder and rapine."[19]

Victor Stenger also weighs in on the Inquisition and its horrific results beginning with the Albigensians of southern France. From there, "Dominican priests devised fiendish machines of torture that were used on thousands in France and Spain."[20] Stenger sets the origins of the Inquisition within the context of the

Crusades. The Crusades had begun at the end of the eleventh century to regain the Holy Land from the Muslims, but Innocent III later decided to declare a crusade back home against the Albigensians. For Stenger, the hunt for heretics was just the first in a series of atrocities committed by Christians: "holy wars, burning of heretics, the Crusades, the Inquisition, the Thirty Years' War, the English Civil War, witch hunts, cultural genocide, brutal conquests of the Aztecs, Incas, and Mayans, ethnic cleansing, slavery, colonialist tyranny, and pogroms against the Jews eventually leading to the Holocaust."[21]

Harris also gives great attention to connecting the dots from the Crusades to the Inquisition to the witch hunts to Jewish persecution and ultimately the Holocaust.[22] These events vividly illustrate the "misery and ignorance" characteristic of not only medieval but all Christian history.[23] Harris makes it clear that the abominations of medieval Christianity may belong to the past, but their root cause of faith and irrationality remain ever within Christianity and any other religion. Change for the better appears in history thanks only to science, rationality, and modernity.

The fourteenth century stands out in Harris's *The End of Faith* as epitomizing all the worst features of medieval Christendom. Just as Christopher Hitchens's children know more than the unfortunate ignorant but pious believers of the past, so Harris imagines that if we could revive a "well-educated Christian of the fourteenth century," he would prove a "total ignoramus" on everything except faith: "His beliefs about geography, astronomy, and medicine would embarrass even a child, but he would know more or less everything there is to know about God." Since that time, of course, we have come to know about all these other matters while faith and ideas about God have apparently remained frozen in their fourteenth-century state: "Religion, being the mere maintenance of dogma, is one area of discourse that does not admit of progress."[24]

Other references to the benighted fourteenth century place it in the darkest of the Dark Ages. Their simple, ignorant faith ill-equipped people to deal with the devastation of the Black Death as it swept through the continent. As a result, they did not know what caused the pestilence. Harris can only comment that such faith blocks reason and the science that would one day produce the penicillin they so desperately needed.[25] When criticizing so-called "moderate Islam," he argues it does not exist or, if it does, "it is doing as good a job of hiding as moderate Christianity did in the fourteenth century (and for similar reasons)."[26] Harris fears what would happen if Muslims got the vote in Iraq, Syria, Algeria, Iran, and Egypt, likening it to "opening the polls to the Christians of the fourteenth century."[27]

Christian reform movements over the centuries and the Reformation of the sixteenth century hold little interest for the New Atheists for two reasons: (1) Christianity, like all organized religion, cannot, and therefore did not, reform itself except when it departed from its core dogma and tagged along with the progress brought about by reason and science; and (2) reform movements only make matters worse. Even St. Francis of Assisi, a favorite of Catholics, Protestants, and many others, wins no nod of approval. Hitchens dismisses him as someone who lectured birds.[28] Harris sums up the saint's life as one that created "yet one more wealthy and corrupt order, to strengthen the hierarchy, and to facilitate the persecution of all who excelled in moral earnestness or freedom of thought. In view of his aims and character it is impossible to imagine any more bitterly ironical outcome."[29]

According to Hitchens, Luther showed some courage in challenging papal authority but went on "to become a bigot and a persecutor in his own right, railing murderously against Jews, screaming about demons, and calling upon the German principalities to stamp on the rebellious poor."[30] Luther warned against reliance on reason, calling it "the greatest enemy that faith has;

it never comes to the aid of spiritual things, but more frequently than not struggles against the divine Word, treating all that emanates from God."[31] His writing against the Jews "probably influenced Hitler."[32]

The second-generation reformer John Calvin established a harsh regime in Geneva that amounted to a form of totalitarian rule.[33] It persecuted dissenters from Calvin's orthodoxy, including the celebrated physician Michael Servetus, burned at the stake for his heresy. Hitchens continues that Calvin belongs with Osama bin Laden and the Inquisitor Torquemada in seeking out and persecuting those guilty of deviant ideas or behavior.[34] No wonder then that Calvinism went on to witch-hunting in Europe and America or later defended apartheid in South Africa.

Harris followed up his *End of Faith* with another bestseller, *Letter to a Christian Nation*, which takes the form of a letter to a member of the "Christian Right." At one point he thunders against both Luther and Calvin for advocating "the wholesale murder of heretics, apostates, Jews, and witches."[35] He cites as his source once again William Manchester's *A World Lit Only by Fire*, but he gives no specific page references.[36] Manchester does have a few pages on how adamant all Protestant regimes were and how Calvin's Geneva "represented the ultimate repression" and had all the marks of a "police state."[37] Unfortunately Manchester has no endnotes in his entire text. Harris and Manchester may think they have it right about Luther and Calvin, but they offer us no evidence to support their portrayal of them.

The Protestant reformers broke with Rome for many reasons, but for Harris, "their treatment of their fellow human beings was no less disgraceful. Public executions were more popular than ever; heretics were still reduced to ash, scholars were tortured and killed for impertinent displays of reason, and fornicators were murdered without qualm." The basic lesson to be drawn from all this was summed up nicely by Will Durant: "Intolerance is the natural concomitant of strong faith; tolerance grows only when faith loses certainty; certainty is murderous."[38]

Within the larger narrative of the New Atheist history, the Protestant Reformation churned up a religious revival throughout Europe that could bode no good. When the papacy awoke to the depth and breadth of the threat posed by Protestantism to its authority, it harnessed reforms still within its fold and launched the so-called Counter-Reformation. The resulting clash of these two great reforming forces only enhanced the most zealous and fanatical adherents on both sides. Europe fell into a bloody period of religious conflict that plagued the second half of the sixteenth and first half of the seventeenth century.

The more moderate and rational path toward reform championed by the so-called Christian humanists got caught in the middle. Erasmus of Rotterdam sought through scholarship and an occasional popular treatise to return the church to its original sources in scripture and the early church fathers. He labored within the educational program begun by Italian humanists the previous century, who looked to the ancient world both pagan and Christian for inspiration and wisdom. Erasmus might have hoped that the obscure German monk from Wittenberg would be an ally in his efforts, but he soon realized he and Luther differed bitterly on how to achieve reform. His call for reasonable and gradual reform that could keep the church unified ran into Luther's stubborn insistence on immediate change even if it meant repudiating the papacy and causing schism. Manchester writes that poor Erasmus "died a martyr to everything he had despised in life: fear, malice, excess, ignorance, barbarism."[39]

Europe fell into a period of religious strife characterized by unparalleled brutality on all sides: "No one has calculated how many sixteenth-century Christians slaughtered other Christians in the name of Christ, but the gore began early."[40] Luther's movement divided the cities and states of the Holy Roman Empire into

Lutheran and Catholic, with the Emperor Charles V struggling to maintain Catholic hegemony despite his differences with the papacy and the threat of the Muslim Turks advancing into his territories and threatening Vienna itself. He finally called it quits with the Peace of Augsburg in 1555 that recognized Lutheran and Catholic cities and principalities in the empire, the religion of each determined by the city government or prince: *cuius regio, eius religio.*

That principle had yet to apply in the rest of Europe. Monarchs did assert their authority over the churches, but they often met with insurgent movements counter to their wishes. After Henry VIII broke with Rome, transforming the church in England into the Church of England, his daughter Elizabeth I had to struggle against not only Catholic threats from abroad but a troublesome minority of Calvinist Protestants at home known as Puritans. The Calvinist movement in France remained a minority, led by Protestant nobles who provided the military leadership for thirty years of warfare. The fighting stopped only when the Calvinist Henry of Navarre assumed the throne and converted to Catholicism, supposedly uttering "Paris is worth a mass."

Thus, by 1600, Europe found itself deeply divided over religion, which complicated the growing rivalry among the major states of the continent: France, the Holy Roman Empire, Spain, and England. The resolution of the religious conflicts in this "Age of Religious Wars" came thanks to the triumph of the secular state over the church in the seventeenth century. Once the state tamed religion, the way opened for intellectual innovation and the emergence of reason in the Scientific Revolution and, beyond that, the Enlightenment of the eighteenth century.

For Harris, it had been a long wait. Europe had marked time for centuries, awash in religion and superstition that impeded reason from bringing on the modern world. He fixes his attention less on where Europe had travelled over the past half millennium and more on what it, and the rest of the world, might have achieved if only the power of reason had unleashed itself and illuminated these dark centuries: "There is no telling what our world would now be like had some great kingdom of Reason emerged at the time of the Crusades and pacified the credulous multitudes of Europe and the Middle East. We might have had modern democracy and the Internet by 1600. The fact that religious faith has left its mark on every aspect of our civilization is not an argument in its favor, nor can any particular faith be exonerated simply because certain of its adherents made foundational contributions to human culture."[41] With breathtaking clarity, Harris manifests his powers of historical analysis in this extraordinary statement.

History 101: New Atheist and Mainstream History

Three constituent elements made up what the textbooks call "Medieval Europe": the legacy of Greek and Roman civilization, the customs and way of life of the Germanic or "barbarian" tribes, and Christianity as embodied in the Latin or Catholic Church. Older texts commonly spoke of the "synthesis" of these three forces in the development of European civilization. Today we tend to see a mix rather than a synthesis, as evidence suggests the three ingredients never formed a coherent whole but rather produced the differences and tensions that marked medieval society. The New Atheists show no awareness of these basic elements of medieval society.

By the third century, the Roman Empire dominated the whole Mediterranean world and much of the European continent up to the Danube and Rhine Rivers, as well as England and Wales. Germanic tribes put pressure on the borders and would push across those borders in the next century, hoping to gain some of the benefits of Roman civilization. Financing and defending the empire became an ever greater task. The lack of an orderly method of political succession led to a parade of emperors in the mid-third century, many of whom emerged from the military. These major internal political weaknesses appeared a century before Christianity emerged as the imperial religion.

Christianity began as a Jewish sect and by the third century had gained adherents in many parts of the empire, principally in cities. Often left alone, they periodically suffered persecution for both their refusal to take an oath to the emperor and their usefulness as a scapegoat when an emperor needed one. The persecutions of the mid- and late third century took a dramatic turn when the Emperor Constantine tolerated Christianity and supported the church. In the late fourth century, Theodosius made Christianity the established imperial religion.

Germanic tribes first defeated an imperial army at Adrianople in 378. Then Alaric and his Goths sacked Rome in 410. The church's greatest theologian, Augustine, wrote his *City of God* in response, differentiating between the City of Man that was always perishable and the City of God that was eternal. In practical and worldly terms, Rome, like any political entity, might perish, but the church would endure so long as it fulfilled God's will. Theodoric, a Germanic chief, succeeded the last of the Roman emperors in 476. When Justinian, the Roman Emperor in Constantinople, sought to conquer the Italian peninsula, it led to the devastating "Gothic Wars" in the mid-sixth century that left much of Italy a wasteland and the city of Rome a shadow of its former self. Into the political vacuum stepped the Bishop of Rome, Gregory I, or Gregory the Great (590–604).

In the western church, Christian monasticism played a key role in medieval society. Benedict of Nursia (c. 480–c. 550), reacting to the licentiousness and fragmentation of Roman society, withdrew to the life of a hermit south of Rome. He attracted so many followers that he formed a community with a common way of life that became the Benedictine Rule. The Rule mixed a life of prayer and work. Monks took vows of poverty, chastity, and obedience in an austere way of life that avoided extreme forms of asceticism.

The western church grew through a mixture of missionary endeavor and conquest. The key to converting a Germanic tribe lay with the chief, who had earned his title primarily through military leadership. If he opted for Christianity, the whole tribe followed. Hence when Clovis decided on baptism at the end of the fifth century, his Frankish tribesmen followed him. In the eighth century, the Frankish descendants of Clovis conquered a series of tribes under the leadership of Pepin and his son Charlemagne. Charlemagne, pious Christian and fierce warrior, finally overcame his most stubborn enemies, the Saxons, slaughtering thousands and pushing the survivors into Christianity.

The stories of Benedict and Charlemagne underscore the ambiguities that took root in Christianity and have shaped so much of its history. The life of prayer, study, and work strove to preserve a core of Christian faith that stressed moderation and peace. The Christianity of Charlemagne paid homage to piety and learning, as evidenced in the illiterate leader's support of learning and preserving texts of antiquity, both Christian and pagan, but it also included the traditional virtues and values of Germanic warriors. The New Atheists choose not to recognize this ambiguity, thus foreclosing any sense of nuance or context in their treatment of European history.

Charlemagne revived the imperial title by having himself crowned Roman Emperor in 800 by the pope. With the eastern empire, what we call the Byzantine Empire, under Greek control, and the Muslim conquest of the Holy Land and North Africa, Charlemagne established his headquarters in northern Europe in Aix-la-Chapelle, modern Aachen. The so-called Carolingian Empire constituted what historians commonly call the "First Europe"—the first distinctly Western European realm.

Charlemagne's empire got divided among his descendants, and then new incursions from the outside further weakened it. The ferocious Vikings or Norsemen sallied forth from Scandinavia to loot, plunder, and pillage. Magyars swept in from the east and got as far as central Europe, while Muslim Saracens attacked Sicily and parts of Italy. The scene finally calmed down in the second half of the tenth century as Saracen raids ebbed, the Norsemen went home or settled in as Christians in Normandy, and the Magyars inhabited the neighborhood roughly of Hungary. A Saxon chief again revived the imperial title as Emperor Otto I in 962. The three strands—Roman, Christian, and Germanic—entwined again in the fabric of Western Europe.

The newly found stability set the stage for the period commonly known as the "High Middle Ages," from c. 1000 to c. 1250. The period embodies what comes commonly to our minds when we think of medieval society: Gothic architecture, knights, chivalry, universities, and so on. Less commonly recognized, but basic to the stability and growth of this society, was an agricultural revolution that used new technology to produce enough food to support a growing urban population engaged in trade and commerce. Europe no longer seemed dark and defensive. By the eleventh century, it found the strength and drive to expand its own borders and to build new and innovative institutions. These developments in medieval society fail to receive even a modicum of attention in New Atheist historiography. The idea that medieval Europe had any dynamic or creative elements remains anathema.

To this day, Europe is dotted with hundreds of churches and cathedrals that rose in this period. Initially the traditional, fortress-like style known as Romanesque predominated, but new building techniques led to the more graceful Gothic style with its soaring spaces and stained glass windows bringing in color and light. Dismissed in the Enlightenment as barbaric, hence "Gothic," these structures stand out as remarkable achievements of human imagination and engineering.

Society had three major constituent groups: the feudal nobility who controlled the main resource, land, which gave them the wherewithal to bear arms and provide military leadership;

the peasants who tilled that land and owed obedience to their noble lords; and the clergy, both monastic ("religious") and parochial ("secular"), supervised by bishops and archbishops who often came from the nobility. Royalty—kings and emperors—came from the nobility, who considered them not absolute monarchs but first among equals. This social and political framework allotted no place to the merchants and traders who increasingly drove the economy and dwelt not on the land but in the cities. The result of all this meant a society static and fixed in theory but dynamic and changing in fact, a point ignored by the New Atheists.

In theory, Christendom, the *respublica Christiana*, constituted a variety of temporal authority unified by a common Christian faith as professed and practiced by the Latin Catholic Church, as differentiated from the Eastern Orthodox Church. In practice, constant tension and conflict erupted between competing temporal and spiritual authorities. The so-called Gregorian Revolution of the eleventh century pitted the claims of Pope Gregory VII (1073–85) against those of the Holy Roman Emperor Henry IV (1056–1106). Gregory's radical idea put the authority of the priesthood, represented by the Bishop of Rome, over that of kings and emperors when the two authorities clashed. Henry had to seek Gregory's absolution to lift his excommunication in the famous incident at Canossa in Tuscany. The victory seemed to go to the pope, but once absolved Henry struck back and Gregory died, isolated and bitter, in exile. The clash of Henry II of England and Archbishop Thomas Becket a century later formed another chapter in this medieval struggle over ultimate authority in Christendom. The political history of the Middle Ages reveals a clash between temporal and spiritual authorities, rather than the papal theocracy of New Atheist fantasy.

The historically controversial Crusades began as a part of the papal revolution. Urban II (1088–99) sought to assert his authority by organizing the reconquest of the Holy Land, taking a cue from the *Reconquista* in Spain where Christians had initiated a counterattack against the Muslims that led to the capture of Toledo in 1085. Sending armies to the east would give a Christian stamp of approval to the growing population of armed knights who caused widespread disorder and bloodshed at home. The church had previously sought to pacify society through such campaigns as the "Peace of God" and the "Truce of God." No doubt Urban thought it made good sense to give these troublesome warriors a holy task that would not only send them away but send them on a mission to rescue Christians suffering under Islamic rule and redeem the Holy Land. As one medieval historian put it, "The Crusades represented a fusion of three characteristic medieval impulses: piety, pugnacity, and greed."[42]

The only non-Christian population tolerated, even if at times barely, were the Jews. They became easy targets for overzealous crusaders ready to attack the "enemy within": "From the start . . . the crusades were marked by depredations and violence which were as much racial as religious in origin. Mass-gatherings of Christians for any purpose invariably constituted a danger to Jewish communities in European cities. Local rulers nearly always tried to protect them for their own selfish financial reasons; but they were powerless to control the vast crusading bands."[43]

The Christian warriors achieved surprising success on the First Crusade, when they captured Jerusalem in 1099 and slaughtered the local population. Over the next two centuries, Westerners launched a series of these military excursions as Christians and Muslims fought for control of the eastern Mediterranean. The Westerners could also turn against their fellow Christians. During the Fourth Crusade, they conquered the Christian city of Zara on the Adriatic coast for the Venetians who were transporting them to the Holy Land. They continued east and conquered the greatest Christian city of all, Constantinople. The papal leadership of Innocent III (1198–1216) also organized the first domestic crusade against the Albigensian heretics in southern France.

The political struggle that took center stage in the thirteenth century pitted popes against Holy Roman Emperors and French and English kings. Innocent III clashed with John of England and Philip II of France. His successors had to cope with the mighty Hohenstaufen Emperor, Frederick II (1215–50). Among the issues dividing the papacy and the so-called Holy Roman Empire, the control of the Italian peninsula stood at the top. Frederick's domination of both central Europe and Sicily threatened the independence of the pope and his rule over the Papal States in central Italy. Control of that territory would ensure papal freedom to exercise its spiritual authority in keeping with the Gregorian ideal of preventing lay control of the church and its clergy.

By the end of the thirteenth century, the popes and emperors had fought to a draw. The bigger threat to the papacy came from the French King, Philip IV, who humiliated Pope Boniface VIII. Boniface had claimed great authority in a series of papal bulls asserting the full range of papal claims to superiority over royal authority, but papal theory fell victim to political and military realities. Shortly after Boniface's death, the papacy abandoned the increasingly violent city of Rome and set up shop in Avignon. To critics, this "Babylonian Captivity of the Church" looked like a papacy dominated by French popes and French interests from 1309 to 1378.

When the papacy did try to return to Rome, it led to disputed elections and rival papacies in Avignon and Rome from 1378 to 1415. This "Great Schism" ended when the Council of Constance managed to push aside the rival popes and unify the papacy under Martin V (1417–31).

In the early thirteenth century, the Dominicans and the Franciscans represented a new type of religious order distinct from traditional Benedictine monasticism. These "mendicant" or begging orders did not live communally in monasteries but had a mobility to move about in society to preach. Dominic (c. 1172–1221) came from Castile, and his friars specialized in preaching as guardians of orthodoxy against heresy. Francis (1182–1226) grew up in a town, Assisi, where his father prospered as a merchant. His religious conversion led him to abandon his hedonistic and disorderly adolescence in favor of a life of poverty dedicated to preaching and service. These two mendicant movements responded to the changing conditions of a European society increasingly wealthy and more sophisticated. St. Francis and his followers represented something beyond the "mammal who was said to have preached to the birds," in the dismissive words of Christopher Hitchens.[44]

The Dominicans and Franciscans soon became rivals. They both developed a strong presence in the growing universities, where they took part in an expanding intellectual world, often opposing one another theologically. The schoolmen or "scholastics" in the universities renewed the debate, going back to the early centuries of Christianity, on the relationship of knowledge derived from reason and that from revelation. The greatest effort to reconcile reason and revelation came from the mind of the Italian-born philosopher and theologian Thomas Aquinas (1204–74). Aquinas ended up on the faculty at the center of medieval theology at the University of Paris. He sought to show that the philosophy of Aristotle could be reconciled with Christian doctrine by demonstrating that reason established basic beliefs such as God's existence, God's unity, and God's goodness, while revelation established doctrines reason could not discover such as the Incarnation and the Trinity.

Thomas's major adversaries were Franciscan theologians who downplayed the role of reason and argued that we are dependent on God's revelation through such means as the Bible for the truths of Christianity. They sowed seeds of suspicion toward attempts to undergird revelation with reason. Reason compromised God's sovereignty. God's will reigned supreme in matters of faith. The Franciscan William of Ockham (c. 1285–1347) rejected any idea that limited God's omnipotence and freedom. At the same time, he developed methods of reasoning and logic, including the famous "Ockham's razor." Suspected of heresy, he fled to the court of the Emperor Louis IV, where he wrote in favor of imperial interests against those of the papacy. The fourteenth century made it clear that the unity of Christendom survived only as an ideal and a dream; in reality, tension, division, and conflict marked the intellectual and political life of Europe.

The standoff between papacy and empire left the Italian communes and cities on their own. Outside of the Papal States, and sometimes within them, the communes now pursued something new in medieval Europe: independence from any higher jurisdiction. By the fifteenth century, the dozens of communes had consolidated into five major territorial powers—Venice, Milan, Florence, the Papal States, and the Kingdom of Naples—and a host of lesser ones. The economic strength of the Italian cities set the stage for the literary and artistic movements we call the Renaissance.

"Back to the sources" served as the slogan of the cultural renewal of the Renaissance. Antiquity had always held a fascination for medieval Europe, but the Italians took a fresh look. As politically independent city dwellers whose wealth derived from commerce and banking, the Italians of the Renaissance had little interest in the metaphysical disputes of the medieval schoolmen or the titanic struggles of papacy and empire over ruling Christendom. They looked back to Rome as the greatest city-state in history, whose letters and arts now served as models to imitate.

Imitation led to innovation. The revival of classical Latin and the search for ancient texts led to new insights into ancient history, literature, the Bible, and the early church. By the end of the fifteenth century, Greek and Hebrew unlocked more of the sources of antiquity. Schools at the courts of Italy used the new learning to train the young in the *studia umanitatis*, the humanities that equipped elite youth for civic duties. New styles of art and architecture used classical models to produce works that sought the ideal of harmony and balance. These Italian cultural developments would soon spread to England and continental Europe.

To govern the relationship of the city-states, the Italians invented modern diplomacy with resident ambassadors, intelligence reports, a sense of secular state interests, and seeking a balance of power among the five major states. Machiavelli (1469–1527) cut his political teeth serving the Florentine republic. In his most celebrated treatise, *The Prince*, he laid the groundwork for a wholly secular understanding of politics devoid of the traditional Christian moral basis for political life.

The papacy played a significant role in the development of Renaissance culture and politics. Pope Nicholas V (1447–53) founded the Vatican Library and encouraged humanistic study. By the end of the century, Rome had supplanted Florence as the cutting-edge patron of the arts, most famously illustrated by the stormy relationship between the warrior pope Julius II (1503–13) and Michelangelo. The Sistine Chapel, named for Julius's uncle, Pope Sixtus IV (1471–84), became the preeminent example of Renaissance art both for Michelangelo's magnificent ceiling and for his Last Judgment behind the high altar, completed several decades later.

The papacy faced an irresolvable dilemma that helps explain the outbreak of the Reformation. Having established their political independence by ruling the Papal States, the popes had to preserve it by all the tricks and maneuvers of Renaissance Italy's diplomacy and war. The more the papacy became enmeshed in Italian politics, the less it appeared able to carry out its primary mission as the moral and spiritual leader of Western Christendom. Combining Christian leadership of Europe with the often petty and nasty politics of Italy posed a dilemma that left the papacy open and vulnerable to harsh criticism and ultimately rebellion.

In the early sixteenth century, the most visible and influential heralds of church reform emerged among the Northern or

Christian humanists, led by Erasmus of Rotterdam. The northerners had their own version of "back to the sources," but they focused more on Christian sources than did the Italian humanists. Erasmus's scholarship produced a new Greek text of the New Testament based on the enhanced knowledge of the original Greek. The revival of Hebrew allowed the Christian humanists to penetrate more authoritatively the Old Testament. Erasmus also produced new versions of several of the early church fathers. The scholarship of Erasmus and his fellow humanists aimed to spark reform of church and society based on the example of early Christian life.

Then the storm broke when an unknown German monk and university professor raised probing questions about church practices that exploded into major controversy and conflict. Martin Luther (1483–1546) nailed his Ninety-Five Theses to the church door in Wittenberg to protest the sale of indulgences that seemed to promise believers that good works, including cash payments, would spring their loved ones out of purgatory. Luther, who had come to a new understanding of the primacy of faith over works, soon became a public figure when the theses were translated from Latin to German and widely disseminated. The Reformation would be the first major movement in European history spread by the new technology of printing.

From the beginning, Luther's protest became entwined with politics and economics. Although excommunicated by Pope Leo X in 1520 and condemned by the Hapsburg Emperor Charles V at the Diet of Worms in 1521, Luther took refuge in a castle under the protection of his prince the Elector Frederick the Wise. Even Erasmus found Luther too much of a bull in a China shop and publicly broke with him. Soon some cities and territories in the Holy Roman Empire backed Luther's vision of reform by rejecting papal authority and implementing Luther's version of the mass. Luther's translation of the Bible into German opened access to it by a growingly literate population. The Bible had primacy of authority, superior to that of popes or councils.

Soon Latin Christendom suffered fractures that would never heal. Lutheranism took hold in much of the German-speaking areas and Scandinavia. Henry VIII's repudiation of papal authority led to the emergence of an independent Church of England under his daughter Elizabeth I (1558–1603). Ulrich Zwingli (1484–1531) disagreed with Luther over doctrinal matters and led his own reform movement in Zurich. Then John Calvin (1509–64) led the most dynamic of the Protestant movements, first in Geneva, but then spreading to France (the Huguenots), parts of the Empire, Scotland, and the Puritan movement within the Church of England.

Protestantism fragmented as it spread, but all Protestants rejected papal authority and came to see the papacy as anti-Christ itself. They agreed on the primacy of scripture and God's gift of grace to those with faith. The failure or success of these movements commonly depended on politics. Political leaders might well be attracted to Protestant ideas, but they might be just as attracted by the prospect of seizing church property or gaining political control of the church with all strings to the foreign Bishop of Rome cut. The New Atheists fail to acknowledge or understand this intermingling of the religious, cultural, economic, and political forces that shaped society during the Reformation period.

How did the popes react to the threat of Protestantism? For a tangle of religious and political reasons, the initial response was hesitant and uncertain. Only during the reign of Pope Paul III (1534–49) did the papacy begin to harness Catholic reform by calling a church council at Trent, recognizing new movements such as the Society of Jesus, and encouraging preaching and teaching that would counteract Protestant efforts. The three sessions of the Council of Trent held from 1545 to 1563 defined and shaped a new, militant Catholicism with the papacy firmly in control.

On every key doctrinal point, the council rejected Protestantism. Newly established seminaries would now educate and train clergy for parish life under the direction of reform-minded bishops.

The religious divisions complicated the diplomatic and military relations of the Europeans in the sixteenth century. For a time Spain emerged as a superpower when the marriage of Ferdinand and Isabella united the kingdoms of Aragon and Castile. The notorious Spanish Inquisition gave the new Spanish monarchy a means to purge heretical and potentially subversive elements among Jews and Muslims, including those who converted to Christianity. Their grandson assumed the throne in 1516 as Charles I, and three years later the seven electors of the Holy Roman Empire elected him the Emperor Charles V. The house of Hapsburg brought together Germany and Spain as a superpower threatening France. The French King Francis I (1515–47) fought a series of wars against Charles. Much of the fighting took place in and over Italy until a peace settlement in 1559. The inspiration for these wars came from the rivalry of these two dynasties, both firmly Catholic in their religion.

Then came the so-called Age of Religious Wars from 1559 to 1648, featuring a series of conflicts over an entanglement of political, religious, and economic interests.[45] The religious divisions of France between the dominant Catholics and the minority Calvinists or Huguenots led to an on-again-off-again set of civil wars over who would control the French throne. When the Protestant Henry of Navarre inherited the throne, he converted to Catholicism and, as Henry IV, began to reestablish royal authority. The Edict of Nantes in 1598 gave the Calvinists judicial and legal rights as well as freedom to worship in designated areas. That opened the way to the renewed assertion of the monarchy that would culminate with the so-called absolutism of Louis XIV.

As Europe entered the seventeenth century, it resembled what Italy had been in the fifteenth century: a congeries of independent states vying with one another for military, territorial, and economic advantage through a system of war and diplomacy. The new century did not mean the end of religion as a major element in society, but it did mean the subordination of religious institutions and practices to the interests of the respective states. Modern Europe had succeeded medieval Christendom.

Issues

I recall giving a lecture in the 1970s in a survey on medieval Europe explaining the sacramental system of the church and in particular the meaning of transubstantiation, according to which the bread and wine in the Mass became the body and blood of Christ. Afterward an undergraduate approached me with some questions that seemed to express disapproval of what she had just heard. As we talked, it struck me that she may have thought I was proselytizing or teaching religion rather than history. I concluded that she would have preferred the history of the Middle Ages with the religion left out.

The New Atheists want a version of medieval Europe that takes the opposite approach: They present medieval Europe with only the religion left in—at least the parts they think will demonstrate the depravity and moral bankruptcy of Christianity. The omission of significant chunks of Europe's past mars the New Atheist portrayal of all historical periods, but it reaches a particularly egregious level in dealing with the Middle Ages. They betray little knowledge or interest in the economic, intellectual, cultural, and political aspects of medieval Europe.

In economic developments, medieval people proved more clever and innovative than the New Atheists' depiction of ignorant boobs living in squalor and quite incapable of inventing anything useful like penicillin to fight plague, pestilence, and disease. Historians of medieval technology point to a number of devices that increased agricultural efficiency, such as improved designs for ploughs and windmills or innovations like the horse collar. The increased production allowed markets to develop that funneled food to cities as the population began to increase in the tenth and eleventh centuries. Some historians talk of an "agricultural revolution" that could sustain the growing urban population. Urban centers in Italy and the Low Countries spurred international trade that stretched from the eastern Mediterranean in an arc up to northwest Europe and England. These developments mark a dynamic, not a static, society.[46]

The universities of Europe and the United States today descend directly from the medieval prototypes in Paris, Oxford, Cambridge, Bologna, and elsewhere. Students flocked to them to prepare for careers in theology, law, and medicine. Although the church played a central role and clergy dominated many of them, the universities maintained a degree of independence that allowed for intellectual innovation and disputation. Hitchens admits the scholastics achieved something intellectually, although he manages to do so in his usual condescending and dismissive language. He grants that their methods just might gain his approval: "We have nothing much to learn from *what* they thought, but a great deal to learn from *how* they thought."[47]

When Thomas Aquinas taught at the University of Paris in the thirteenth century, he labored to construct a philosophical and theological system that incorporated Aristotle's philosophy with Christian theology. His work frightened more conservative theologians, who accused him of heresy. Nevertheless, Aquinas and his work survived, albeit with considerable opposition. Only later, after the sixteenth-century Council of Trent, did Thomism become officially supported as the main system of Catholic thought, a position it maintained until the Second Vatican Council in the twentieth century.

Thomas Aquinas stood in a long line of Christian theologians, going back to Augustine and the early church fathers, who searched for ways to connect Christian doctrine to the intellectual milieu of the day. He wanted to answer the same questions they had posed: What does Athens have to do with Jerusalem? What does man's reason have to do with God's revelation? Aquinas found a way to reconcile the two in a way that did not deny reason but incorporated it into a Christian framework. His fellow Dominicans favored his approach while the rival Franciscans rejected it.

Historians, of course, do not take sides in such disputes. Their task remains as always to include important and significant developments in history that will help us to understand any given period of the past. Medievalists, therefore, commonly see the thirteenth and fourteenth centuries as seminal in forming a foundation for modern intellectual history, including the emergence of modern science. They cite, for example, the work of such figures as Robert Grosseteste (c. 1170–1253) and Roger Bacon (c. 1212–94). The latter, a Franciscan at the University of Oxford, dabbled in all sorts of ideas and speculations that included championing the necessity of experimentation. Today's historians of science debate how and why modern science would ultimately come forth in a Christian society, but no matter where they come out with their interpretations, they do not ignore or omit the intellectual history of the Middle Ages in their quest for understanding, as do the New Atheists.

The New Atheist historians stand outside this debate, as they already "know" that Christian faith and superstition had killed science and reason centuries before, and only with Copernicus in the sixteenth century would science resume: "Had Christianity not interrupted the intellectual advance of mankind and put the progress of science on hold for a thousand years, the Scientific Revolution might have occurred a thousand years ago, and our science and technology today would be a thousand years more advanced."[48] Science apparently disappeared with the triumph of the Christian Church, only to reappear out of the blue with the work of Copernicus's *De revolutionibus orbium caelestium* in 1543.

When it comes to the political history of the Middle Ages, the New Atheists do not bother with the significant and fascinating role of the rulers who dominate the works of historians, such as Frederick I "Barbarossa" and Frederick II "Stupor Mundi" of the Holy Roman Empire, or Philip II "Augustus" of France, or Henry II, John, Edward I, and Edward III of England. By leaving them out, the New Atheists indulge themselves in berating the papacy for its crimes while they mislabel medieval politics as "theocratic." Harris mentions in passing the "theocratic terrors" of medieval life.[49] Victor Stenger brushes aside Charlemagne in favor of considering "the popes who were the true rulers of Europe in the centuries known as the Dark Ages (curiously coincident with Christendom) and whose motives can surely be attributed, partly or wholly, to religion."[50] That opens the way to offering examples of great crimes of medieval popes while omitting the key conflict of medieval politics between the spiritual authority of the church and the political authority of kings and emperors. No historian of the medieval period agrees with Stenger that the popes were "the rulers of Europe," nor do they label the period from c. 500 to c. 1500 the "Dark Ages."

Reason and consistency require that words have precise meaning as historians employ them in exploring the past. *Theocracy* means rule by those who claim immediate divine guidance. Medieval popes would not have understood the term, but they pushed for an authority derived from divine authority that anyone may accurately see as theocratic. The central point of mainstream historians' account of medieval Europe is that the popes failed because of the opposition of secular powers that grew in strength and power as the period progressed. The popes had enough trouble trying to control the European church, let alone controlling the political rulers as well: "Distances were too great and ecclesiastical egos too tender for the pope to become the great puppeteer of the European Church. And secular rulers were much too strong to permit anything resembling a papal theocracy."[51]

During the fourteenth and fifteenth centuries, the papacy proved no hindrance to the secular rulers of the day and the development of the institutions by which they ruled. The off-again-on-again wars between England and France, known to us as the Hundred Years War (1337–1453), required increased revenue to fight them. The clergy and nobility commonly resisted efforts to pull more cash out of them. As leaders in society and as counselors to the kings, they began to form the rudiments of representative bodies. This period contained the origins of England's parliament, which would take on a new prominence in sixteenth-century Tudor government. Dismissing the fourteenth century as a time of ignoramuses and boobs whose religious knowledge prevented them from making progress leads to a distorted history that falls short of an intelligible and intelligent view of the past. The New Atheists pick out what they consider constitutes all the bad stuff of the Middle Ages, assuming that nothing good or worthy of our attention could possibly come out of a society dominated by superstition. Universities, parliament, trade, improved agriculture, and sundry other topics languish in obscurity during their portrayal of these centuries of abominable Christian domination.

The cultural and literary history of medieval and Renaissance Europe merits no attention from the New Atheists. Harris's depiction of the bleak fourteenth century peopled by hopelessly ignorant people leaves out any mention, for example, of Dante (1265–1321) and Petrarch (1304–74). Dante may have shared in the religious "delusions" of his contemporaries, but he doubtless qualifies for Harris's definition of a "well-educated Christian of the fourteenth century." That excellent Christian education meant, unfortunately, that he was a "total ignoramus" on everything else. In the next generation, Petrarch and Boccaccio (1309–75) continued to embarrass themselves by their abysmal ignorance, although historians normally point to their other achievements. Such blustering by the New Atheist historians may give them satisfaction, but it fails once again to fall within the boundaries of historical discourse.

The New Atheists skip over the Renaissance and its new perspective on the relationship of Christianity with antiquity so they can get on with pointing out the absurdities of Protestant reformers like Martin Luther and John Calvin. Luther's suspicion of reason, outbursts against the Jews, and fears of the rebellious German peasants form the core of what we need to know about the German monk. Any historians of the Reformation will include those points in presenting Luther. The difference between them and the New Atheists lies in their efforts to set these words and actions of Luther's within the context of his age rather than chastising him for not being more like Harris, Dawkins, Hitchens, and their friends. The goal of Reformation historians, as of historians in general, remains that of understanding the past in terms appropriate for each period. Such historical understanding does not excuse history's protagonists for what we find morally objectionable, but it does mean avoiding fits of moralistic condemnation as substitutes for historical inquiry.

The moralism of the New Atheists also manifests itself in the linking of Luther and Calvin to modern atrocities. In Luther's case, it means making him a causal agent of the Holocaust. Thus Dawkins quotes Luther in his *On the Jews and Their Lies* that "all Jews should be driven from Germany." He adds that Luther's words "probably influenced Hitler." Dawkins then makes a great leap forward of five hundred years to show to his satisfaction that Luther and Hitler shared the Christian faith and its hostility to the Jews.[52]

Hitchens drops Calvin into the twentieth century as a totalitarian ruler. The argument seems unique to Hitchens and is not found among mainstream historians. For example, Abbot Gleason's useful and well-received survey, *Totalitarianism*, fails to mention Calvin's Geneva as "a prototypical totalitarian state." Gleason's only mention of Luther comes in connection with a discussion of the work of German historian Gerhard Ritter. At one point Ritter suggested that the totalitarian state could be viewed as a process begun with the Christian Middle Ages, but, Gleason concludes, Ritter laid the ultimate blame for the totalitarian possibility in Europe on the "appearance of the masses on the historical stage during the French Revolution. Their gullibility and lack of preparedness ultimately made totalitarian dictatorship possible in nations."[53] The point is not whether Ritter's interpretation is correct. The point is that he and other modern historians do not ascribe the totalitarian concept to sixteenth-century Protestant reformers.

Robert Daniels expresses a typical mainstream view of Soviet totalitarianism in contrasting it with traditional autocratic, monarchical authoritarian rule: "The totalitarian system, which imposes its controls and demands on the entire citizenry and in all walks of life, is a twentieth-century phenomenon, relying on modern developments in communication, weaponry, and record keeping." It is a revolutionary attempt to undo the status quo and remold society.[54] Hitchens's crude attempt to link the regimes of Stalin, Hitler, Mussolini, Mao, and others in the twentieth century to the Protestant leaders suffers from his anachronistic technique of casting modern evils on his historical targets of opportunity.

The New Atheists present their favorite subjects as though they were the only subjects that counted in European history from the medieval period through the Reformation: the Crusades, the Inquisition, witch hunts, and religious wars. Most of us share with them moral outrage at many aspects of these historical phenomena. That does not excuse the New Atheist historians from their sloppiness and imprecision in dealing with them.

The Inquisition, for example, had a medieval version, a distinctly Spanish version beginning in the late fifteenth century and a renewed Roman version instituted by the most unattractively militant pope of the sixteenth century, Paul IV (1555–59). Most popular visions of the Inquisition have Spain in mind, especially as presented by H. C. Lea's *A History of the Inquisition of the Middle Ages* (1888). In recent decades, a number of historians have offered fresh studies of all forms of the Inquisition that give us a better understanding of what went on.[55] Again, the purpose is clarification, not exoneration. In the case of Spain, the Inquisition begun in the late fifteenth century became a tool of Ferdinand and Isabella's state as it went about purging Spain of alien and subversive elements. As usual in this period, religion and politics were very much entwined, a basic condition overlooked in New Atheist historiography.

Victor Stenger mounts a blitzkrieg of charges on Crusades, Inquisition, witch hunts, and religious war that throws around statistics of those victimized in these undertakings, but with no clear indication of his sources for this information.[56] He informs us that the Thirty Years War turned "Europe into a wasteland," with Germany's population dropping from 18 to 4 million "according to one estimate," but he does not bother with the source of that or any other estimate. Stenger informs us that the Albigensian Crusade massacred "an estimated two hundred thousand to one million people . . . ordered by Pope Innocent III" but again fails to cite a source. Historians know of the devastation of the Thirty Years War and the bloodshed of the Albigensian Crusade, but Stenger ought to at least cite sources and try to "get the story straight" before tossing about numbers.

Stenger gives away the game in his review of the Albigensian Crusade when he continues in the same paragraph with the information that "Stalin killed perhaps ten million from a Soviet population many times greater than that of southern France in 1209, so Innocent III was a far greater criminal than Stalin if you consider the percentages." He adds in a footnote, "Some scholars believe that figure [for Stalin] was greatly inflated by cold war propaganda."[57] He leaves it to his readers to guess who these scholars are.

Historians have pinned many labels on Innocent III, not all of them favorable, but Innocent as worse than Stalin breaks new ground. New Atheist history's unique quality stems from its ability to find new perspectives that have escaped mainstream historians. Condemnation by comparison across the centuries usually does not fit with the historian's task, and for good reason: It makes no sense in understanding either party. By dragging Innocent III from the thirteenth to the twentieth century and setting him beside Joseph Stalin, Stenger sheds light on neither Innocent nor Stalin and the times in which they lived, although he does reveal something about his perverse way of exploring history.

Innocent III did confront the secular rulers of his day in his bid to carry out the mandate of the Gregorian reform that the church maintain an independence from the control of laymen, no matter how exalted their titles. In the longer run, as we have seen, the papacy failed in that effort. Historians agree that by the seventeenth century, the growing strength of European states subordinated the church and the clergy to state policy: "The secular authorities were everywhere firmly in charge of organized religion, as they had been during the earliest stage in the Reformation, 1517–1540, before the religious wars began. Europe was covered by a network of territorial churches—some Catholic, some Protestant, but all managed by the state and subservient to the state."[58]

Italian historian and philosopher Benedetto Croce reminded us that "all history is contemporary history." Historians agree that our concerns, interests, and perspectives morally and politically play a role in shaping our views of the past. The issue as always is, to what degree should our contemporary attitudes determine the history we produce? When we decide to arrange the past with the express purpose of using it to support our present agenda, we deny any possibility of history as an autonomous discipline bound to adhere to particular methods intended to yield some truth about the past. Historians should acknowledge their biases, interests, and perspectives and then do their best to set them aside. Otherwise, history becomes hopelessly subjective, subject to whatever current cause we favor. We then forfeit any chance of finding common ground in examining the past, regardless of our political or religious beliefs. The New Atheist historians have chosen an errant path to the past. They apparently do not recognize that in doing so they turn their backs on the Enlightenment and the evidence-based reasoning they constantly champion.

CHAPTER 4

Back to the Present
History In and Out of Bounds

> The idea that any one of our religions represents the infallible word of the One True God requires an encyclopedic ignorance of history, mythology and art even to be entertained.
>
> —Sam Harris[1]

On April 11, 2000, the verdict finally came after months of testimony and cross-examination. It took the form of a 350-page judgment handed down by Judge Charles Gray in the British high court. Judge Gray's ruling exonerated the defendant, American historian Deborah Lipstadt, from the charges of libel brought against her by David Irving, English writer and historian. British libel law differs markedly from United States libel law. It heavily favors the plaintiff, who does not have to prove malicious intent, and thus makes it incumbent on the defendant to prove that what she said or wrote is truthful. In this unusual case, history itself seemed to be on trial, although it ended up exposing the shoddy historical methods of Mr. Irving in his numerous books on Nazi Germany and World War II.

How did these two historians end up facing each other in court, and what were the central issues that led to Gray's judgment? The 62-year-old Irving had published some thirty books as an adept, self-trained, independent historian, laboring outside the confines of the academic world. Fluent in German, he had a facility for finding documents and sources unknown or neglected by others. His collective rendering of the Third Reich favored the Germans, but in a manner that some historians thought had the merit of giving us insights into the mentality and thinking of Germany's political and military leadership.

Irving published his first book in 1964 on the *Destruction of Dresden*, telling the tale of the devastating Allied bombing of the beautiful baroque city in eastern Germany in February 1945, shortly before the war's conclusion. He placed his array of statistics on civilian deaths and the city's obliteration within a scenario that cast doubt on the Allies having any legitimate military purpose for the raid other than placating the advancing Soviets. His vivid writing helped make the case for Dresden as an Allied atrocity.

The robust sale of subsequent books gave Irving the resources to live well in London and pursue his research and writing as an independent historian. Some of his interpretations and conclusions began to raise red flags among historians. His sympathetic portrayal of Hitler in *Hitler's War* (1977) included the assertion that Hitler had not ordered the mass extermination of the Jews and only learned about it in 1943. Irving later set out to demonstrate in his biography of Josef Goebbels in 1996, *Goebbels: Mastermind of the Third Reich*, that the Nazi propaganda chief, not Hitler, had set in motion the campaign to destroy the Jews. By this time, Irving had identified himself with the leading Holocaust denial organization, the Institute for Historical Review, attending several of its annual meetings. In 1990, he gave the featured address during the same conference that heard John Toland.

The Goebbels biography caused a very public and heated controversy when St. Martin's Press cancelled plans to publish an American edition in the face of protest and pressure from the outside. Christopher Hitchens entered the fray by condemning St. Martin's for reneging on the book contract. His article in *Vanity*

Fair characterized David Irving as "not just a Fascist historian" but also "a great historian of Fascism." On the Charlie Rose television program, Hitchens called Irving a "necessary historian," although he failed to clarify what he meant. Hitchens denounced Holocaust deniers and acknowledged that he would have no quarrel with St. Martin's if it had decided against publishing the Goebbels biography initially, but he found their caving into outside pressure reprehensible.

Deborah Lipstadt entered the Irving drama in 1993 with her book *Denying the Holocaust*. She laid out the history of Holocaust denial and how deniers falsify history. She argued that they no more deserved time on college campuses to present their historical fabrications than did members of the Flat Earth Society to present theirs. Her book mentions Irving frequently. Lipstadt considers him particularly dangerous because he presents himself as a genuine historian seeking objective truth about the past, when his work suggests the contrary: "Irving is one of the most dangerous spokespersons for Holocaust denial. Familiar with historical evidence, he bends it until it conforms with his ideological leanings and political agenda."[2] Her statements furnished Irving with the evidence he needed to take her to the British high court for libel.

The trial took four months and its details need not detain us. The expert witness for Lipstadt's defense, historian of the Third Reich Richard Evans, wrote a fascinating account of the proceedings, *Lying about Hitler*.[3] Irving took charge of his own defense but failed to convince Judge Gray that he pursued history objectively, albeit with some sympathy for the Germans. Irving no doubt hoped to convince the judge, as well as the wider audience following the trial, that the core of his work contained valuable historical insight into Germany, Nazism, and the war, even if some of his opinions caused controversy. Some historians had said as much, giving Irving's work credibility, while arguing that he had veered off course when it came to Hitler and the Holocaust.

Evans disagreed with this generous assessment of Irving and devoted a chapter of *Lying about Hitler* to showing how Irving's ideology shaped his work from the beginning of his writing career. The chapter deals with testimony during the trial about Irving's first book, *The Destruction of Dresden*. In that book, Irving inflated the number of civilian casualties, concealed evidence he had to the contrary, and only reluctantly revised the numbers downward several decades later in a revised edition of the book. Evans makes clear that he and most historians do not defend the destruction of Dresden, "but the way to reach a reasoned judgment on these events was not to falsify the evidence, which was already horrifying enough: all that did was to obscure the real issues."[4]

Our chief concern with this trial focuses on the reasons given for exonerating Deborah Lipstadt and denouncing David Irving. The judge found that Irving acted as an "active Holocaust denier." As reported in *The New York Times*, "The judge, Charles Gray of the British high court, handed a resounding victory to Ms. Lipstadt. In a scathing ruling notable for its stern wording, he declared that Mr. Irving was a racist Holocaust denier who deliberately distorted historical evidence in order to cast Hitler in a favorable light. Mr. Irving's treatment of history, he said, was often 'perverse and egregious.'"[5] Judge Gray further charged that "Irving has for his own ideological reasons persistently and deliberately misrepresented and manipulated historical evidence."

Irving had violated the historian's obligation not to distort evidence for ideological reasons by quoting out of context, omitting contrary evidence, and presenting his personal speculations as fact. Even so, Gray declared, these conclusions did not justify on their own the defense's case. The defense had further to show that Irving deliberately distorted the past for ideological purposes. On that score, Gray stated that "in my view the Defendants have established that Irving has a political agenda. It is one which, it is legitimate to infer, disposes him, where he deems it necessary, to manipulate the historical record in order to make it conform with his political beliefs."[6]

The Irving case demonstrates that some versions of history fall outside the boundaries of authentic history. The rendering of history must rest on evidence that historians can then assess and debate. Abiding by the rules and methods of good historical practice is an obligation of all historians, whether academic or independent. Writers who ignore that obligation and allow their current ideological concerns to shape the past place themselves outside the discipline of history as developed since the Enlightenment.

I am not linking the New Atheists directly to the substance of Holocaust denial, but I am charging them with acting like a gaggle of polemicists and ideologues who misconstrue history for present purposes. We have the same objection to those who portray the American Civil War as the "War of Northern Aggression," in which slavery had no part in bringing about that conflict. The same goes for those offering elaborate historical scenarios to show that America began as a "Christian Nation" and should be so recognized today. No doubt the New Atheists would agree that all three of these examples represent bad history. Nevertheless, they employ many of the same flawed techniques to make their case that historically religion has been the major evil force in history that "poisons everything." Their method of doing history puts them in some very suspect company.

The History of History

To set the context of New Atheist history, we need to look briefly at how the discipline of history developed over the centuries, especially since the Enlightenment. The New Atheists claim to stand in the tradition of the Enlightenment and apparently agree with Hitchens in his call for a new Enlightenment. It is important to see if they abide by the original Enlightenment when it comes to writing about history. This overview of the history of history as a discipline provides the necessary context for putting the New Atheist version of the past outside the boundaries of accepted historical practice.

Humans love to tell stories, including stories about the past. Such stories in the form of myths and legends often explained the origins of various aspects of the world around us, natural and human. When the Greek writers Herodotus and Thucydides in the fifth century BCE sought to tell the stories of great wars and conflicts using credible sources for accuracy, they blazed a path ultimately leading to the modern discipline of history. Both men departed from the dominant cyclical way of thinking reinforced by myths, legends, and fables in a search to understand politics and warfare by studying history.[7]

The later Roman historians built on the Greek legacy, also concentrating on politics and war as the central subjects of history. The Roman historians injected moral judgment into their histories. Titus Livy's *History of Rome* championed civic virtue, and Suetonius's *Lives of the Caesars* offered vivid portrayals of emperors, warts and all. Julius Caesar wrote a military memoir that gave us plentiful observation and considerable detail on his campaigns in the Gallic Wars. Tacitus, considered by many as the greatest Roman historian, exposed immorality and corruption at the center of Imperial Rome, as contrasted with the virtues of the Germanic tribes who had defeated Roman legions.[8]

Not surprisingly, the Christian church offered its own version of history growing out of the Jewish tradition. The Jews and Christians viewed history as a straight line running from Creation to the Final Days and the coming of the Kingdom of God. The Christian Bible begins with the creation stories in Genesis and culminates with the Last Judgment in Revelation. The Christian "master narrative" puts Jesus's birth as the central fact of history, hence a calendar dated before and after that event. Medieval maps placed Jerusalem at the center of the world.

St. Augustine made a distinction between sacred and profane history, the city of God and the city of man, with his greatest interest focused on the former. Ultimately history moved teleologically—that is, toward the end or *telos* ordained by God and guided by his Providence.⁹ The Augustinian historical scenario dominated medieval thinking about history, but the Renaissance brought a shift in the interests of urban Italians to the worldly, secular activities of life, grounded in commerce and politics. Renaissance figures looked for inspiration to the world of antiquity, both pagan and Christian. They invented a view of the past that stands firm in history textbooks to this day: Antiquity, the Middle or Dark Ages, and the Renaissance as the modern rebirth of arts and letters inspired by ancient examples.

Renaissance humanist history turned away from universal, Biblically based themes to examine the history of particular cities. The Florentines, for example, produced a number of histories of their city, including Machiavelli's, in the early sixteenth century. History also served to teach lessons for current political life. Machiavelli used ancient history freely in *The Prince* (1513), believing that he could apply that history directly to his day. His younger compatriot Francesco Guicciardini rebuked Machiavelli for assuming that political lessons from antiquity could apply to the Italy of their day. His own *History of Italy* focused on contemporary history beginning in 1494, when Italy suffered invasions from the French and then the Spanish.

A major humanist contribution to the development of critical history, based on the evidence yielded by sources, came from their understanding of philology, the development of language over time. Lorenzo Valla, despite having a job in the papacy, demonstrated what others had only suspected in his *Discourse on the Forgery of the Alleged Donation of Constantine*. The Donation of Constantine purported to be a fourth-century document whereby Constantine ceded considerable authority to the pope when he moved his imperial headquarters to the east and his new namesake city of Constantinople. Based on an analysis of the language, Valla showed that it more likely dated from several centuries later as the papacy sought to assert its authority. His scholarship undercut a major source used to authenticate papal claims to temporal authority.

The northern or Christian humanists led by Erasmus also sought to learn from the past by going back to the sources of early Christianity in the Bible and the early church fathers. Although Luther and Erasmus disputed one another over what path to take to reform the church, they shared the belief that scripture and the primitive church pointed the way. As both Protestant and Catholic reform movements developed in the sixteenth and seventeenth centuries, both sides probed early church sources to justify their positions. The resulting publications constituted milestones in the collection of documentary sources that then formed the basis of critical history.

The Enlightenment of the eighteenth century laid the intellectual foundation for the modern world that would include the subsequent emergence of the modern discipline of history. Voltaire's contribution came in his reflections on the philosophy of history and his own historical masterpiece, *The Age of Louis XIV*. History, however, did not hold the key to the change and reform he championed for his own society. The critical use of reason would bring about progress. History could help by showing how the modern world emerged from the barbarism and superstition of the past. The idea of progress thus became a hallmark of Enlightenment thinking, but it had the negative effect of distorting the past in the name of that progress. "Voltaire, for example, was notoriously unable to recognize any good in the Middle Ages; his historical writing traced the growth of rationality and tolerance and condemned the rest. So, if the desire to demonstrate progress is pressed too far, it quickly comes into conflict with the historian's obligation to re-create the past in its own terms. In fact historicism took shape very much as a reaction against the present-minded devaluation of the past which characterized many writers of the Enlightenment."[10]

Edward Gibbon labored over twenty years to produce the greatest historical work of the century, *The Decline and Fall of the Roman Empire*. He covered a period of more than a millennium that climaxed with the fall of Constantinople in 1453. He relied for sources on the work of seventeenth-century historians and antiquarians. His unique achievement was a massive narrative that synthesized the vast content of those sources. Gibbon shared the Enlightenment's displeasure with religion, superstition, and priest-craft. Hence his interpretation of what went wrong with the Roman Empire placed heavy blame on Christianity. Gibbon's great achievement also revealed the weakness of Enlightenment scholars that later historians condemned: "They had failed to carry out the historian's primary task, that is, to elucidate the past, not merely to condemn it."[11]

The great advance toward the modern discipline of history came in the course of the nineteenth century, beginning in Germany. German scholars set new standards by basing their historical work on documents preserved in archives. Archival research continues to this day as the mark of the professional historian. The documents of any particular period constitute the primary sources on which historians base their articles and books. Those products of the historian's pen become in turn the secondary sources that the rest of us read when we want informed presentations of past subjects.

The greatest figure in the nineteenth-century school of German historiography was Leopold von Ranke (1795–1886). He established the university seminar for the training of advanced students in the critical study of sources, which later became the model for university graduate training in the United States. While Ranke had his own Prussian and Protestant biases, he emphasized the ideal of objectivity by establishing the facts and then putting them in their proper context. The historian must show how things actually were, "*wie es eigentlich gewesen.*"

Ranke realized that, in the words of a later historian, "the past is a foreign country, they do things differently there."[12] He asserted the importance, therefore, of "historicism" (*historismus*), meaning that the historian must take the bold but necessary step into the world as viewed, understood, and lived by those inhabiting that past. Only in that way could he gain some understanding of any period in the past. "What was new about the historicists' approach was their realization that the atmosphere and mentality of past ages had to be reconstructed too, if the formal record of events was to have any meaning. The main task of the historian became to find out why people acted as they did by stepping into their shoes, by seeing the world through their eyes as far as possible by judging it by their standards."[13]

History developed in the nineteenth century during a period of great advances in science, technology, and medicine that fed the sense of human progress. The traditional focus on politics, diplomacy, and warfare continued as new interests emerged. Nationalism fostered the search for national identity through the history of language and culture as well as politics. Industrialization inspired economic history and the study of economics itself. Social history explored the inner workings of society in its social groups and institutions.

The widening scope of inquiry into the workings of human society encouraged the social sciences: economics, sociology, anthropology, and psychology. These disciplines influenced historical research and began the often fruitful, sometimes contentious, relationship of history to these new disciplines. Scientific method provided the foundation for all of them in guiding them toward truth as sure and certain as the truth yielded by the natural sciences. In his inaugural address as Regius Professor of Modern History at Cambridge in 1902, J. B. Bury (1861–1927) declared that history "is herself simply a science, no less and no more."[14]

Historians today commonly beg off making predictions about the future by declaring "there is no future in history." Nineteenth-century scholars exuded more confidence in spelling out the future prospects for humankind. Scientific and technological progress assumed a concomitant moral progress that would usher in a better future in general. The philosophy of positivism exemplified this optimistic vision of the future. Positivists sought to validate historical knowledge through adherence to scientific methods, especially empiricism, which would yield the laws of historical development similar to the scientific laws of nature and the universe.[15] The sociologist Auguste Comte (1798–1857) confidently laid out his Law of the Three Stages, showing the evolution of the human mind from the theological to the metaphysical to the positive.[16]

Karl Marx (1813–83) based his overview of historical development on a materialist philosophy that in some ways resembled a secular version of a Christian view of history. Social and political relationships rested on a foundation of material conditions involving who controls the means of economic production and the labor force. Change came when the conditions had changed sufficiently so that a new dominant class formed. In Europe's medieval, agrarian past, the feudal landholding class ran the show, based on the labor of serfs. With the growth of industrialization and commerce, a middle class, the bourgeoisie, came to control commerce and industry with a proletarian working class. Political revolution took place when the new class supplanted the older one. Thus the classic French Revolution brought the downfall of the feudal order and the rise of the bourgeoisie who then took the reins of political power. Now the time was coming when the proletariat would rise up to overthrow the bourgeois order in a revolution that would lead to a classless society. History and its laws of change replaced Providence and led to a utopian future here on earth rather than in some pie-in-the-sky heaven.

For Marx, religious and political institutions formed the superstructure of society, resting on the foundation of material and economic stuff that determined what lay above. Marxist and non-Marxist economic interpretations gained currency by the dawn of the twentieth century. Non-Marxists might not buy completely into Marx's superstructure image, but they commonly stressed the importance of underlying economic forces in determining what the protagonists of history said and did.

Sigmund Freud (1856–1939) revolutionized the understanding of human psychology. The power of the subconscious in human motivation had a marked influence on twentieth-century historians, especially after World War II. Psychohistory became fashionable, producing fascinating biographical sketches of major figures, from Martin Luther to Adolf Hitler. Erik Erikson's psychology of adolescence and the stages of human life informed his influential portrait of *Young Man Luther* (1958). During World War II, the OSS (Office of Strategic Services), predecessor employed Walter C. Langer to produce a psychological analysis of Hitler that later saw the light of day as *The Mind of Adolf Hitler*.

Freud himself had indulged in speculative history with his books *Civilization and Its Discontents* and *Moses and Monotheism*. These books affirmed the strong scientific bent of the nineteenth century. Religion, according to Freud, belonged to the childish past. Modern man should abandon such delusions and face life in the modern age. The problem with Freud's psychological and historical reflections, and their use by the practitioners of psychohistory, was that they are not subject to verification. The initial claims of psychohistory dissolve in the face of critical evaluation. Freud's techniques of psychological diagnosis of patients did not work well with dead subjects.

A more successful use of psychology was as one aspect of the Annales school of French historians that emerged between the two world wars. They downplayed the significance of individuals and events typically featured in traditional historical narrative. They wanted to probe below that surface to reveal the underlining determinants of history by using geography, sociology, psychology, economics, and cultural anthropology. They stressed how the fundamental determinants shaped history over the long haul, or what they called the *longue dureé*. In proper historicist fashion, they searched for the *mentalité* of any given period—that is, the attitudes, assumptions, and ideas that permeated a culture. Understanding the *mentalité* would thus help us traverse the past as a foreign country.

Marc Bloch's two volumes on *Medieval Society* broke new ground by covering geographical, economic, social, and cultural forces before a narrative of personalities and events. In the next generation, Fernand Braudel's (1902–85) magisterial study of *The Mediterranean and the Mediterranean World in the Age of Philip II* followed the same pattern. Braudel seemed to cover the geography of every inch of the Mediterranean coastline and the resulting economic and social conditions. Only in the end of his lengthy study did he get around to Philip II, Spain, and what took place in the late sixteenth century.

In the late twentieth century, the influence of the social sciences on historians shaped a generation of social historians eager to explore people and places neglected by most traditional historical writing. The slogan "history from the bottom up" signaled a reaction against the "top down" study of politics, diplomacy, and war as carried out by "elites." Much overdue attention went to women, working people, minorities, and the marginalized. Often emulating the *Annaliste* methods, these historians began with underlying conditions before proceeding to the story of particular groups in particular periods.

For example, Emmanuel Le Roy Ladurie studied peasant life and rural civilization in medieval southern France. His book on *Montaillou* (1978) quickly became a classic, telling the story of the Inquisition's search for Albigensian heretics in the early fourteenth century. Thanks to the meticulous records kept of the interrogation of suspects by the local bishop, the book reconstructed the everyday life of peasants in Montaillou, including their religious and magical observances and even their sex lives. "As Le Roy Ladurie puts it, the high concentration of Cathar heretics in Montaillou 'provides an opportunity for the study not of Catharism itself—that is not my subject—but of the mental outlook of the country people.'"[17] Carlo Ginsburg made a similar study of the beliefs of an early seventeenth-century miller in northeastern Italy, also based on Inquisition records, in his *The Cheese and the Worms*. Both of these books presented cases of "microhistory" with the aim of illustrating and illuminating the society in which each took place.

At the other end of the historical spectrum, attempts to discover some overarching framework for the unfolding of history, or master narrative, continued well into the twentieth century. Marxists still saw the path to the modern world in revolutions that transitioned from one period to the next. Social scientists produced an impressive theory of modernization, predicting that traditional societies would have to pass through stages to modernization similar to what had happened in the West. Oswald Spengler (1880–1936) came up with a more pessimistic assessment of the way history was going after World War I in his *The Decline of the West*, resurrecting "the cyclical view of history" that "saw no means of escape from the dictates of destiny." He analyzed the various "cultures" of the past such as the Babylonian, Chinese, Classical, and so on, with each passing through phases of life from birth to death.[18]

It takes some imagination today to recall the impact of Arnold Toynbee (1889–1975) on the English-speaking world after World War II, when he came up with his own scheme of the rise and decline of civilizations throughout history. An Englishman of great erudition, he wrote a multivolume work, *A Study of History*, akin to Spengler's efforts but with significant differences. In a two-volume abridgement, it became a bestseller. "In Toynbee's analysis, civilizations took shape when demanding challenges brought forth creative human responses."[19] Some civilizations died while others such as the Western, Islamic, and Hindu survived. When Toynbee did not quite know what to do with civilizations that did not fit well in his overall scheme, he called them "fossilized" relics, as in the Jewish and Buddhist traditions. Not surprisingly, many critics took exception to his grand sweep of history, and today his work is largely forgotten.

Hedgehogs know one big thing, Isaiah Berlin taught us, while foxes know many small things.[20] Most historians fall more in the fox than the hedgehog camp, which is why they resist grand master narratives in history. It is usually not hard to find empirical evidence that undermines the big theories. Historians strive for objectivity, even if the discipline lacks the certainty we associate with scientific methods. The most recent challenge to objectivity in historical writing came out of postmodernist literary theory.

Postmodernists argue that language and texts shape reality, including historical reality. Furthermore, historians' own predilections shape their historical texts and represent their ideologies and political allegiances. There looms an element of power that supports the "hegemonic" groups in society. Language, text, and aesthetics reign over notions of substance and objectively verifiable truth. To put it succinctly, the postmodernists challenge the legacy of the Enlightenment, arguing that "there can be no objective historical method standing outside the text, only an interpretive point of address fashioned from the linguistic resources available to the interpreter."[21] Consequently, postmodernists reject not only the grand master narratives of the hedgehogs but also the monographs of the archival foxes as bearers of objective truth.

As they have done with other intellectual trends in the past, historians have come to value and absorb, up to a point, some of the salient features of postmodernism. Historical writing is literary, but it is not fiction. The present viewpoints of historians shape to some degree the history they produce, but that does not rule out the existence of a knowable past beyond the words of the text. We know that history is commonly written by the "winners," who may distort or omit the history of subordinate groups. Nevertheless, history has its own self-correcting methods of seeking evidence and context to widen perspectives so that even the "losers" come under view. History's unique function goes beyond its linguistic, literary, and aesthetic qualities. Otherwise we would have nothing to learn from the past.

Historicists point to the existence of a knowable past, even if we can know it only approximately. We know that we cannot live in the past nor recreate it except vicariously. Our human nature gives us a common bond of understanding with the people we study, at the same time we acknowledge that they live in a foreign country. Hence we have the basic task of establishing historical context. As G. M. Young (1882–1959) suggested, we need to read ourselves into a period until we can hear its people speak.[22] "Respect for the historicity of the sources is fundamental to the historical project."[23]

John Tosh lists three requirements for historians to fulfill their task of reconstructing the past.[24] First, they must take a hard look at their own assumptions, values, and sympathies, and how they relate to their subject of study. Self-knowledge is a desirable trait for historians, and they do themselves and their readers a service by spelling out in a preface or introduction how that may connect with their writing. Second, historians must be prepared to change or adjust their initial hypothesis as a result of the evidence they uncover. "It is sometimes forgotten by non-practising [sic] critics that much of the excitement of historical research comes from finding results which were *not* anticipated and pushing one's thesis into a new direction." Third, historians must put their work into historical context as they make every effort to avoid "presentism." They must avoid the cardinal sin of any historian, which is anachronism, or reading the present into the past. Tosh's three points are strikingly similar to the three points made by J. H. Hexter several decades before.[25]

New Atheist Historiography

In their abstract devotion to reason, the New Atheist historians stand firmly on the side of Enlightenment values and the possibility of verifiable truth. Unfortunately, their historical practices veer toward a more subjective viewpoint, failing to measure up to the requirements of Hexter, Tosh, and mainstream historians. They resemble Isaiah Berlin's hedgehog who knows one big thing—in this case, that history shows that religion poisons everything. The New Atheists would do better to find common ground with others, regardless of their beliefs, in exploring the past and debating its meaning within the boundaries of the established methods of historical study.

Dawkins set me on the path that eventually led to the writing of this book. When first reading *The God Delusion*, I stopped on this statement: "I do not believe there is an atheist who would bulldoze Mecca—or Chartres, York Minster or Notre Dame, the Shwe Dagon, the temples of Kyoto or, of course, the Buddhas of Bamiyan."[26] What about the twentieth-century campaigns of communist states to destroy religious institutions, believers, and their churches, such as that initiated by the Soviet Union from Lenin to Khrushchev in the name of a state-imposed atheism? How could Dawkins not know what even a casual reader of twentieth-century history knows? As we have seen, his clumsy attempts to deal with Stalin and religion fail to convince us as historically valid.[27] This piece of historical legerdemain does not stand as a lone instance of making a mistake. It is not a case of a factual slipup or a different interpretation. Rather, it fits as one piece in a pattern of the bad history put out by the New Atheists and their allies.

Professional historians must stick to the sources, especially primary sources, when writing their articles and books. Other writers who wish or need to incorporate history in their work usually turn to secondary works written by well-established and credible historians. The New Atheist writers fall into the second category of relying for the most part on secondary works with occasional printed primary sources. Unfortunately, they fail to do it well.

In the endnotes and bibliographies of the New Atheists, the first notable problem is missing sources. Given the great amount of space they devote to historical arguments to assault religion, it is remarkable what a small, often dated, list of sources they use. They cite very few historians with sound reputations, and they manage to misread, misrepresent, or neglect some of the better ones they do use.

In the case of Stalin, Dawkins employs the tactic of replacing sources with his personal conjectures and dubious logic. How, he exclaims, could atheists like Stalin destroy people and property or start wars "for the sake of an *absence* of belief?"[28] Yes, he acknowledges, Stalin did some evil deeds, but in the name of "dogmatic and doctrinaire Marxism," not atheism. He omits what any textbook would tell him: Marxism included atheism as a piece of its secular ideology that claimed a basis in scientific thinking originating in the Enlightenment. Is it possible Dawkins does not know this? To complete his analysis, he quotes one of his favorite authorities, Sam Harris in *The End of Faith*, who "so often, hits the bullseye [sic]." In this case, Harris supposedly gets us back on target with remarks on the "danger of religious faith" that form a curious conclusion to Dawkins's discussion of Stalin and Hitler. In a kind of incestuous historiography, the New Atheists enjoy citing one another as historical authorities.

Some of Dawkins's sources for Hitler look more interesting because at first glance there are more of them. Nevertheless, some, such as John Toland's *Hitler: The Definitive Biography*, have dubious value. Sam Harris did list an excellent book on Hitler, the first of Ian Kershaw's two-volume biography, *Hitler, 1889–1936: Hubris* (1998), although he never cites it or gives evidence that he used it in his book.

Dawkins turns to Anne Nicol Gaylor, "founder and president emerita" of the Freedom From Religion Foundation. We previously met her in Chapter 1, where she attributed Stalin's misdeeds to his brief time of study in an Orthodox seminary. Her piece on "Hitler's Religion," cited by Dawkins, dwells on Hitler's Catholicism, declaring that "he was a Catholic until his death." She strings together several quotations of Hitler's over the years that she believes support her view that he "regarded himself as a Catholic until he died." She also cites John Toland to the effect that Hitler was "still a member in good standing of the Church of Rome, despite detestation of the hierarchy."[29] The game here aims to avoid any discussion of Hitler's ideology and its sources in favor of presenting him as no more and no less than a Catholic.

Dawkins's other web source cites "Religion and the Holocaust" by Richard E. Smith, whom we also encountered in the first chapter. Smith's amateur status as a historian manifests itself in his list of bullet points on Hitler with no context for them. Smith provides an example of a web source that would not pass muster on an undergraduate paper. Quoting and citing people whose only apparent credential is their agreement with your point of view carries no weight in understanding and assessing historical issues.

Harris does make use of a splendid book by John Glover, *Humanity: A Moral History of the Twentieth Century*.[30] Glover writes more as a philosopher and ethicist than a historian. He is the director of the Center of Medical Law and Ethics at King's College London. He puts together a fascinating and compelling book on our troubled twentieth century, beginning with Nietzsche and covering a myriad of morally challenging topics including Hiroshima, My Lai, Rwanda, both world wars, Stalin, Hitler, and the Holocaust. He interweaves ethics with the "empirical dimension" of history in an informative and sensitive appraisal of the moral disasters of history's bloodiest century.

Harris cites Glover a number of times on various issues, including World War II aerial bombings, the My Lai massacre in Vietnam, and the prospects for world government. He also uses quotations of Nazi leaders Rudolf Hess and Heinrich Himmler as given in Glover. Then Harris attempts to turn the communist ideology of Stalin and Mao into "little more than a political religion" by stating in an endnote that Glover "strikes the same note," but he fails to give any specific references.[31] There is a lively discussion and debate among historians and political scientists about the concept of "political religion" as it applies to modern dictatorships and totalitarian regimes, but there is no evidence that Harris has read their work. His only purpose is to make a secular ideology into a religion.

Harris omits citing or quoting Glover's presentation of these ideologies. It would not fit New Atheist history to quote Glover as follows: "Communism, the major sustained attempt to put an extreme version of the Enlightenment into practice, was a human catastrophe. This was not because of some peculiarities of Stalin or of the people of the USSR. The pattern of the disaster, under Stalin, Mao and Pol Pot, was too similar for that." He then goes on to list the "central defects" shared by all these communist movements.[32] He acknowledges that the rigidity of this ideology "came from religious commitment to the cause," but his overall analysis never confuses a secular ideology rooted in the Enlightenment with traditional religion, as Harris and allies repeatedly do.

Glover also fails to conform to Harris's insistence on placing Hitler in the camp of Catholicism and Christianity. Hitler was not an atheist, but that is not the issue. Glover presents Hitler as "passionately hostile" to Christianity but nevertheless not wanting "to educate anyone in atheism": "A Nazi was encouraged to be a *Gottgläubiger*, a believer in God, but the term carried no suggestion of Christianity. SS members were encouraged to leave the churches."[33]

Harris either missed or suppressed those parts of Glover, as well as this summary of the roots of Nazi ideology: After World War I, "the sense of national humiliation was fertile ground for Nazism. The Nazi project of national renewal gave many people beliefs and the hope of glory. Its belief system was a mixture of Social Darwinism and ideas from Nietzsche. Social Darwinism gave 'scientific' authority to tribalism and from Nietzsche came a belief in will, strength and power, together with a rejection of Judeo-Christian morality."[34] A glance at the endnotes to this chapter in Glover on "The Core of Nazism" reveals a list of several authoritative works by established historians on Nazi racial, medical, and scientific practices. He did his homework.

In his final chapter, Glover offers this observation: "Those of us who do not believe in a religious moral law should still be troubled by its fading. The evils of religious intolerance, religious persecution and religious wars are well known, but it is striking how many protests against and acts of resistance to atrocity have also come from principled religious commitment."[35] The question is not of whether Glover is correct on every point but of why Harris misrepresents his book.

New Atheist supporter Richard Carrier wrote a scholarly piece, published in the *German Studies Review* in 2003, that called into question the translation of some of the quotations of Hitler used by Glover. The thrust of Carrier's article was that poor and inaccurate translation made Hitler sound more anti-Christian than in fact he was.[36] He makes a good case and shows the perils and pitfalls of getting at exactly what Hitler may have said in his "Table

Talk," when his off-the-cuff remarks were recorded by others. Carrier overreaches, nevertheless, when he states, on the basis of the 1933 Nazi concordat with the Vatican, that "there can be no doubt that the Nazis were thoroughly and devotedly Christian, eager to inculcate Christian theism for future generations." He also cites David Irving as a source and remarks in a footnote that "Irving is infamous as a 'holocaust denier,' though in truth he does not deny the holocaust happened, only that Hitler knew of it." Carrier might be expected to be more careful in statements about Irving after the results of his libel suit against Deborah Lipstadt in 2000.

Incidentally, Carrier has played a prominent role among the "mythicists" who argue that Jesus never existed as a historical figure but only as a myth.[37] Bart Ehrman addressed the question of Jesus's existence in his recent book, *Did Jesus Exist?* He reviewed a wide range of evidence and offered a critique of the work of Carrier and other mythicists. He concluded that Jesus did exist and is "best understood to have been an apocalyptic preacher who anticipated that the end of the age was coming with his own generation."[38] Ehrman writes as an historian of the New Testament and the early church. As a self-proclaimed agnostic, he has no stake in the atheist–theist debate. Carrier reviewed Ehrman's book on his blog. He condemned it as "filled with errors, logical fallacies, and badly worded arguments. Moreover, it completely fails at its one explicit task: to effectively critique the arguments for Jesus being a mythical person. Lousy with errors and failing even at the one useful thing it could have done, this is not a book I can recommend."[39]

The argument over Jesus as historical figure or myth need not detain us, although both Dawkins and Hitchens suggest his existence is highly questionable.[40] What stands out for our purposes is Carrier's vehement, no-holds-barred attack on Ehrman, which is consistent with the more adamant New Atheists who seem to take offense at anyone who dares to disagree with them. Ehrman responded and a blog war ensued, with a host of mythicists attacking Ehrman and defending Carrier. Ehrman found it difficult to debate the issues in a rational way that avoided personal attacks on the main protagonists.[41]

In his presentation of Hitler, Dawkins cites two important books by Alan Bullock, one of the giants of twentieth-century European history: *Hitler: A Study in Tyranny* and *Hitler and Stalin: Parallel Lives*. Dawkins offers four endnotes to the two books in a discussion of Hitler and Stalin. Those references are mixed in with ones already noted to Anne Nicol Gaylor and Richard E. Smith.[42] Here we encounter the sheer quirkiness of Dawkins as historian in putting together, on apparently equal footing, a major scholar of these twentieth-century leaders and their regimes with two ill-informed ideologues.

Dawkins treats Bullock as Harris treats Glover: He omits Bullock's conclusions about Hitler and Stalin that undercut his own point of view, implying that Bullock shares his point of view. Bullock tells his readers that the two dictators rejected Christianity and Judaism, that a "Marxist regime was 'godless' by definition," and that Hitler declared conscience a "Jewish invention." He furthermore declares that both men shared "the same materialist outlook, based on the nineteenth-century rationalists' certainty that the progress of science would destroy all myths and had already proved Christian doctrine to be an absurdity." Yes, Hitler's own myth portrayed him as an agent of Providence, and he once stated that the Russians were entitled to attack their priests but they were wrong to reject the idea of a "supreme force." In the long run, Bullock concludes, both regimes aimed to get rid of traditional religion.[43]

Harris and Dawkins betray an inability or an unwillingness to use historical sources properly. They use weak and worthless sources alongside strong and authoritative ones. Then they misrepresent the latter by what they choose to include or omit. Their common ideology explains why. Glover and Bullock reach similar conclusions to one another but have no apparent dedication to a common cause. Bullock wrote as a historian, while Glover selected good historians to guide him in his moral appraisal of the twentieth century. Their conclusions spring from the mainstream of twentieth-century historiography. Dawkins and Harris operate outside that mainstream. They offer no reasons that we should trust their observations on the past.

Harris also appealed to the controversial book by Daniel Goldhagen, *Hitler's Willing Executioners*.[44] Goldhagen's thesis of German "eliminationist anti-Semitism" set off a storm of controversy. It was that rarest of publishing phenomena: a doctoral dissertation that became a bestseller. Goldhagen boldly claimed that Holocaust scholars had gotten it wrong and that he had discovered the true reason for the German destruction of the Jews: the development in the nineteenth century of a new, virulent form of anti-Semitism that called for the physical destruction of the Jews, "eliminationist anti-Semitism." The book received plaudits in media book reviews while meeting with critical rejection from many scholars of the Holocaust.

Harris finds Goldhagen useful because it suits his larger purpose of fitting the modern, secular racism of Nazism into the traditional anti-Semitism of Christianity. For Harris, the anti-Christian Nazi movement "inherited" the anti-Semitism of the church stretching back to the Middle Ages.[45] Harris does not delve deeply enough into Goldhagen's book to show us that he understands the full dimensions of its thesis or why it evoked such strong rejection from a host of historians. As one commentator pointed out, Goldhagen's book surely told us something about the state of the debate on the Holocaust in the 1990s, "thus becoming more than a thesis about history but a fact of it."[46]

Some of the attacks on Goldhagen took on a personal, *ad hominem* quality or involved passionate responses from scholars he had attacked in his book. We need not delve into that morass of charges and countercharges. Nevertheless, a wide range of Holocaust scholars here and in Europe found Goldhagen's thesis unfounded and untenable. Raul Hilberg concluded that "Goldhagen will be quoted by ignorant generalists who are not even aware of the progress made with the opening of archives and the opportunities now beckoning to interested researchers. Thus the cloud that Goldhagen created will hover over the academic landscape. It will not soon disperse."[47] Ruth Bettina Birn struck a more positive note in rejecting Goldhagen's book: "So far, all of the experts in the area of the Holocaust, regardless of their personal background, have been unanimous in severely criticizing Goldhagen's book. That this is the case, fifty years after the fact, and on such a highly emotional and complex subject, is a very hopeful sign."[48]

One of the more judicious and fair-minded appraisals that acknowledged some achievements by Goldhagen, but listed some of his book's deficiencies as judged by standard historical criteria, came from the pen of Omer Bartov. Bartov, Professor of History and German Studies at Brown University, wrote the review that appeared in *The New Republic* on April 29, 1996. Bartov's article is helpful here because many of the deficiencies he highlighted in Goldhagen's work bear a striking similarity to the deficiencies found in the New Atheist historiography.

Bartov finds Goldhagen's claim of originality wanting, because Goldhagen offers a new version of the traditional and largely accepted understanding that traditional anti-Semitism in Christian Europe made the Holocaust possible. Nevertheless, "anti-Semitism as such is not a sufficient condition for explaining the specific nature of the Nazi-attempted genocide of the Jews." It may be the beginning of the story, but it is not the end. Furthermore, Goldhagen fixes his attention on one central cause, the "eliminationist anti-Semitism" that crystallized in the nineteenth century, and then assembles evidence to support it and ignores evidence to the contrary. Bartov comments, "No single element can explain this terrible phenomenon." Historians do not like abstract and monocausal explanations for specific events.

Most telling is Bartov's argument that what Goldhagen presents fails "as an historical explanation of a specific event" and therefore "is useless, and not really historical at all." Goldhagen's central argument that the Holocaust happened because this form of anti-Semitism infected the whole German population "cannot be sustained by evidence, and like all essentialist views it does not require evidence; it is inimical to strictly historical analysis." Bartov continues by asking, what "was it that made the Holocaust a wholly unprecedented event in human history *and* an event which was part and parcel of the specific historical conditions from which it evolved?" Mass killing, he adds, is hardly new, but what was new was modern, industrialized killing carried out by a modern state and supported by its law-abiding and patriotic citizens. What induced leading scientists, legal scholars, physicians, and others to promote and participate in a vast project "that made the concept of transforming humanity by means of eugenic and racial cleansing seem so practical and rational?" Bartov concludes his review with this observation: "Goldhagen is actually appealing to a public that wants to hear what it already believes. By doing so, he obscures the fact that the Holocaust was too murky and too horrible to be reduced to simplistic interpretations that rob it of its pertinence to our time."[49]

My objection to the New Atheists' historiography echoes the objections Bartov levels against Goldhagen, especially presenting one cause as the main or only cause of crimes committed in the name of Nazism. As Bartov says of Goldhagen's book, "no single element can explain this terrible phenomenon." We know that centuries of Christian anti-Judaism and the vulnerability of Jews as the only barely tolerated minority in Christian society forms the historical background to the Holocaust. Furthermore, we know that Christians reacting to Hitler's racial war against the Jews included supporters, perpetrators, and those who looked the other way, as well as a minority who sought to protect the victims. Nevertheless, the Holocaust did not take place solely because of traditional Christianity or some abstraction called "religion." On the contrary, Nazism came from a modern movement dismissive of Christianity and bent on fulfilling the vision of an Aryan racial utopia claiming a scientific basis.

The Nazi fascination with eugenics has obviously given that so-called science a bad name and thus fogged our historical memories of how progressive eugenics appeared when the twentieth century dawned. To understand the Holocaust, scholars have had to go beyond traditional anti-Semitism. The New Atheists ignore the work of those scholars and hence truncate the study of the Holocaust. They believe they know the truth and no more needs to be said or studied concerning it.

In similar fashion, the New Atheists insist on labeling Stalin and company as leaders of a "political religion" for the sole purpose of placing Marxism and communism in the column of religion rather than science. They ignore or omit examination of the origins and salient features of Marxism and its claims to have scientifically unlocked the laws of history. The result was a secular faith that sought to eliminate traditional religion while ushering in a utopian society by destroying any group, institution, or individual standing in the way. Explaining horrendous atrocities, from state-induced mass starvation in the Ukraine in the 1930s to the killing fields of Cambodia in the 1970s, by reference to the poisonous nature of "religion" or vague references to "dogma" hardly qualifies as history for any useful purpose other than trashing religion.

The New Atheist version of history before the twentieth century fares no better. The biggest and most obvious flaw in its historiography stems from the failure to incorporate the major political, intellectual, and cultural forces emerging in Europe in the several centuries before 1900. In particular, they seem at a loss to know what to do with the secular state and the secular ideologies emerging after the French Revolution and the Enlightenment. They enjoy mentioning some of their favorite people, such as Pierre Bayle, Voltaire, David Hume, Benjamin Franklin, Thomas Paine, and T. H. Huxley, but appear uninterested in relating these figures to the larger picture of modern society. The main theme appears to be the importance of this group in encouraging progress toward the modern world over the objections of traditional religion.

In New Atheist history, lack of mainstream books and articles covering European history from the Roman Empire to the Enlightenment is striking. The absence of credible sources leaves the New Atheists free to indulge in a finger-wagging, moralistic kind of history that is not conducive to helping us understand the past. Consider the way Harris, Dawkins, and Hitchens trash Blaise Pascal. They are not alone. There is even a website, "The Rejection of Pascal's Wager: A Skeptic's Guide to Christianity," that fits into the New Atheist way of doing history. For example, on the subject of "Hitler, Stalin and Atheism," it assures us that although Stalin, Mao Zedong, and Pol Pot were atheists, "the primary influences that led to their atrocities were not atheism *per se* but their dogmatic Marxism and communist ideas." They give no hint that one of those dogmatic ideas was atheism and the desire to be rid of religion, nor do they mention regime policies to eliminate religious belief and practice.

Hitchens and even more so Harris vehemently denounce the foolish folks of the fourteenth century as though they stood guilty of the plague, pestilence, war, and famine they suffered. Once again, the problem is not that Hitchens and Harris failed to write a detailed history of medieval, Renaissance, and Reformation Europe but that they failed to use reliable sources and evidence for any period of history when they invoke history to condemn religion.

They might have strengthened their case by doing some homework on the topics they favor in their zeal to reveal the historical horrors perpetrated by the church in the Crusades, the Inquisition, witch-hunting, and religious wars. Historians have produced many well-researched books on these and related subjects in recent decades. These studies have set off fresh debates about how to understand these particular developments within the larger picture of European society. A number of books on the Crusades have appeared in the past two decades that have engendered fresh discussion and intense debate over their causes and nature. The same is true for what historians call the "Witch Craze" that rather suddenly appeared in Western Europe around 1450 and continued for several centuries.[50] There is no evidence that the New Atheists have read or even noticed such modern sources.

A central piece of the Enlightenment master narrative features the greatness of antiquity, the Greco-Roman legacy. The Roman Empire came undone as Christianity undermined its foundations and ushered in the long period of religion and superstition. As Charles Freeman's book argues, the triumph of Christianity meant the end of reason, and Richard Carrier concludes that if Christianity had not put "the progress of science on hold for a thousand years, the Scientific Revolution might have occurred a thousand years ago, and our science and technology would be a thousand years more advanced."[51] Current scholarship, however, suggests some different perspectives.

Not surprisingly, the exaltation of Rome coincided with the apogee of the British Empire of the Victorian and Edwardian periods. British classical scholars and the curricula of leading English public (i.e., private) schools tended to overlook potentially negative aspects of Rome's greatness. Today, scholars like David Mattingly are taking a new and closer look at some of the harsh realities of Roman rule and exploitation of subject populations. Where new lines of historical investigation will lead is not yet clear, but they seem to challenge the more romantic views of an ancient world where reason, justice, and good government prevailed.[52]

The point is not that the New Atheists are wrong and the professional historians are right on any particular interpretation or understanding of the past. Rather, the New Atheist assumption of fixed and static historical positions compares poorly with historians conducting open, ongoing research in order to refresh and improve our understanding of history. The New Atheists fail to engage history seriously in their zeal to support their ideological convictions.

To a large degree, the principal New Atheists under scrutiny here—Dawkins, Harris, Hitchens, and Stenger—justify their alarmist views of religion's influence as necessary reactions to the threat of Islamic jihadism since September 11, 2001. They and their defenders might argue that even if they mess up some of the details of Western history, the major enemy confronting us today is Islam. Harris devotes a major portion of his book to the subject, the other three less so, but all agree on the centrality of the Islamic threat as Harris presents it. As we might expect, however, Harris's sloppy and simplistic way of doing history carries over to his treatment of Islam.

Jackson Lears of Rutgers University specializes in American political and cultural history. In an article reviewing the work of Harris and Hitchens, he notes the "revival of positivism in popular scientific writing."[53] He defines positivism's Golden Age as falling between the Civil War and World War I with its unbounded faith that science could and would produce an explanation for everything, based on the assumption that science alone yields valid truth. That assumption, he believes, laid the foundation for Social Darwinism, popular notions of progress, scientific racism, and imperialism. "These tendencies coalesced in eugenics, the doctrine that human well-being could be improved and eventually perfected through the selective breeding of the 'fit' and the sterilization of the 'unfit.'" Unfortunately, the twentieth century turned out to be a catastrophe that included eugenics being used as a tool by the Nazis to eliminate the "undesirable." Lears notes the distorted views of Harris and Hitchens on Western history and the nature of Islam. Although Harris criticizes others for "an encyclopedic ignorance of history,"[54] Lears points out that Harris's "books display a stunning ignorance of history, including the history of science." His criticism of their misguided efforts includes some of the same issues raised here and provides further evidence for the conclusion that New Atheist history equals bad history.

According to Lears, Harris bases much of his view of Islam's history and current state on the "Manichaean moralism" of Samuel Huntington's thesis about the "clash of civilizations" between Western and Islamic civilizations. Harris accepts Huntington's argument "uncritically, with characteristic indifference to historical evidence." His "tunnel" vision leads him to overlook the roots of radical Islam in modern developments in portions of the Arab world. Islamic "civilization" extends far beyond the particular nations that have given birth to jihadism. Lears agrees with William Pfaff's reminder that lumping together the members of a global religion into one civilization at war with the West "is a Western fantasy."

Lears locates Harris's positivism within his espousal of "the Enlightenment master narrative of progress, celebrating humans' steady ascent from superstition to science; no other sort of knowledge, still less wisdom, will do." Harris's characterization of religion comes off as clumsy at best, betraying an "absolutist cast of mind," and repeatedly reveals historical ignorance. Lears notes that in Harris's discussion of Buddhist meditation, the one religious practice he admits to tolerating, he also shows "his thoroughgoing ignorance of Western intellectual tradition."

Steven Pinker takes offense at Lears's article as an attack on science.[55] He defends his own views that science has brought us a safer world[56] and complains that "a demonization campaign impugns science for crimes that are as old as civilization, including racism, slavery, conquest and genocide." Pinker rips into the humanities for not yet having recovered from "the disaster of postmodernism, with its defiant obscurantism, dogmatic relativism, and suffering political correctness." No one reading Pinker's article and his quotation of Lears would have the faintest idea that Lears had raised significant historical points in a review of several books by Harris. Although Pinker issues a "plea for an intellectual truce" between science and the humanities, it sounds more like a demand for unconditional surrender, as Pinker concludes that "the worldview that guides the moral and spiritual values of an educated person today is the worldview given to us by science."[57]

Hitchens's major contribution to the issue of radical Islam has been his vocal and persistent use and defense of the term *Islamofascism*. The term has received support from those who most vigorously defend the decision to invade Iraq, including Hitchens, and who have pushed for armed confrontation with any perceived Islamic threat. Historians have long grappled with the problems caused by the frequent and loose use of the term *fascist* to label one's political enemies when most of them confine its use to the regimes and movements between the two world wars. Attaching the fascist label to other movements beyond the interwar period usually tells us more about the people using it than it does the subjects so labeled. Hitchens typically ticks off a list of characteristics that he thinks apply to both Islam and fascism, but despite his strained attempts to identify militant Islam with the movements of Mussolini and Hitler, the term does nothing to enhance our understanding of the history and identity of Islam or fascism.[58]

Chris Hedges points out that Harris, Hitchens, and Dawkins "know nothing about the Middle East." They have no command of Arabic, nor do they present any evidence of having studied Islam and Islamic societies. Notwithstanding their ignorance, they use the fear of Islam as a pretext for their own ideas: "They costume their fear and desire for revenge as a war of ideas, a 'clash of civilizations,' and a noble 'crusade' against the pernicious force of religion. And in this clash only one belief system has any validity—their own. Once religion is banished we will all be safe." Hedges reminds us that suicide bombings and other terrorist activities did not originate in Islam but among "secular anarchists in the nineteenth and early twentieth centuries."[59]

We might dismiss the deficiencies of New Atheist historiography if they applied only to the original trio of Harris, Dawkins, and Hitchens, but as we have seen, these three do not labor alone in exploring the past. A varied and polyglot group shares both their methods and substance in doing history. Some are part of that vast field of bloggers whose credentials come more from the passion and certainty of their opinions and less from any particular training or skill in reading history. Others, however, have well-established reputations as leading scientists and intellectuals who may or may not have much interest in history per se but who defend the historical generalizations of the New Atheists.

Prominent physicist and New Atheist ally Steven Weinberg provides an example in a piece in the *New York Review of Books*.[60] Much of the article offers an interesting discussion of the tension he sees between science and religion. He acknowledges that the "conflict thesis" of Andrew Dickson White's *A History of the Warfare of Science with Theology in Christendom* has fallen into disfavor among many historians of science, but he makes the case that the tensions between science and religion still exist and should be taken into account.

Weinberg follows this discussion with an acknowledgment of the New Atheist authors plus some of his own gratuitous historical observations. He informs us that his purpose in the article is not to "argue that the decline of religious belief is a good thing (although I think it is), or to try to talk anyone out of their religion, as eloquent recent books by Richard Dawkins, Sam Harris, and Christopher Hitchens have." He does argue that we do not need religion in the future or its substitutes, such as those in the last century—Hitler's Germany, Stalin's Russia, Mao's China—"that while rejecting some or all of the teachings of religion, copied characteristics of religion at its worst: infallible leaders, sacred writings, mass rituals, the execution of apostates, and a sense of community that justified exterminating those outside the community." His suggested cure is that "we should get out of the habit of worshipping anything." That hews to the standard line established by those "eloquent recent books," but it wanders over the line of responsible and informed historical discourse in trying to make us believe that somehow religion lay at the root of twentieth-century atrocities and avoiding any consideration of the secular and scientific roots of Nazi and Soviet ideology.

Weinberg has also made an observation that now appears as a well-established piece of New Atheist folklore. Dawkins, for example, quotes Weinberg as a follow-up to his assertion that atheists would never bulldoze a religious structure: "As the Nobel Prize-winning American physicist Steven Weinberg said, 'Religion is an insult to human dignity. With or without it, you'd have good people doing good things and evil people doing evil things. But for good people to do evil things, it takes religion.'"[61] Neither Dawkins nor Weinberg offers any scientific way to determine who the "good people" and the "bad people" are. If one could establish both of these types in history, presumably then one could search for empirical evidence in support of Weinberg's dictum. The statement gains one's attention with its catchy phrasing, and it has obvious appeal for those who attribute most, perhaps all, evil to religion or substitutes for religion that are, well, religiouslike. Real historians deal all the time with the vexing question of why people did what we consider evil for reasons they believed were true, honorable, and moral. They know that trying to answer such questions is neither simple nor easy, but such questions are important because they just may shed some light on even history's darkest episodes and thus on the human condition.

Jonathan Glover quotes Alexander Solzhenitsyn in *The Gulag Archipelago* on the troublesome subject of the evils humans inflict on one another: "If only it were all so simple! If only there were evil people somewhere insidiously committing evil deeds, and it were necessary only to separate them from the rest of us and destroy them. But the line dividing good and evil cuts through the heart of every human being . . . it is after all only because of the way things worked out that they were the executioners and we weren't."[62]

A recent example of how Weinberg's pithy put-down of religion has seeped into the wider culture comes in well-known lawyer and author Vincent Bugliosi's vigorous case for agnosticism rather than atheism.[63] Bugliosi's *Divinity of Doubt: The God Question* is destined, according to the book jacket, "to be an all-time classic that sets a new course amid the explosion of best-selling books on atheism and theism—the middle path of agnosticism." Bugliosi paraphrases Weinberg's words with a "someone once said . . . ," apparently unable to track down the source.[64]

Bugliosi attacks Harris, Dawkins, and Hitchens for lacking good arguments for atheism. He charges Harris and Hitchens with not even making a proper case, as they mistakenly seem to think that by discrediting religion and faith they have proven that God does not exist. He thinks better of Dawkins for explicitly arguing for atheism but finds his arguments weak. The only rational position, Bugliosi proclaims, rests with agnosticism.

Even as he attacks the New Atheist trio, Bugliosi mimics in style and substance much of what they put forward to discredit religion and Christianity, including their faulty history. He writes with the same confidence and certitude we have encountered in the others, interspersing his text with such comments as "there can be no dispute" or "we *know* to be a fact, one that cannot really be contested."⁶⁵ He presents a number of opinions on historical topics that bear a striking similarity to the New Atheists on Pascal, Stalin, Hitler, the Enlightenment and its heroes, the Crusades, the Inquisition, the Catholic Church, and religion as a major cause of violence and bloodshed. He even quotes John Toland.

Bugliosi candidly admits to his own insufficiency as a student of history on certain matters and amply demonstrates that insufficiency beyond a reasonable doubt. His handling of historical evidence in the case of Stalin and Soviet policy toward religion offers a splendid example. "But everyone knows," he asserts, "that in the movement toward communism led by Lenin and a young Stalin . . . atheism was but an ancillary tenet to the main engine of the movement—the redistribution of wealth through a class struggle that would bring about the collapse of capitalism."⁶⁶

He then presents as sources three lengthy biographies of Stalin, triumphantly noting that "atheism" only appears in one, in a five-word sentence. He concludes with a rhetorical flourish: "Does anyone believe that the tens of thousands of Soviet citizens who died in Stalin's gulags or were murdered in his purges suffered their fate because of religion?"⁶⁷ Many mainstream historians, including the three he uses here, would answer "yes," that many of those tens of thousands did die as a result of Soviet religious policy. One suspects that Bugliosi never got beyond reading the index in each of these three books, let alone wading through the texts of these or any other books in order to understand the place of religious persecution and state-sponsored atheism in the USSR from its inception to its collapse.

One of his three sources, Robert Service's *Stalin: A Biography*, already furnished a quotation on this subject in Chapter 1. In another passage, Service had this to say: "The first Five-Year Plan was accompanied by vicious campaigns against religion and the Red Army and the 25,000ers arrested clerics and kulaks with equal eagerness. Religion was to be stamped out. Many churches, mosques and synagogues were shut down. Out of 73,963 religious buildings open before 1917, only 30,545 were allowed to function by April 1936 . . . The League of Militant Godless was given sumptuous funding."[68] According to another historian, "In 1939, by which time some 80,000 Orthodox priests, monks and nuns had lost their lives, there were 200–300 churches open in the USSR."[69]

In one paragraph, Bugliosi manages, first, to falsify history when he blithely states, "Most of the anti-atheism [sic] policy of the Soviet state was confined to means like propaganda, and much more rarely, physical destruction of church property." Second, he goes on to falsify the sources he would have you believe support his pseudohistory, such as Service's biography of Stalin. In language harmonious with New Atheist orthodoxy, he lets us know that "the tyranny of Christianity and Islam throughout the ages was *all* about religion, whereas the tyranny of Hitler and Stalin, as well as Mao Zedong, had nothing to do with religion." Bugliosi, like his New Atheist targets, may refer to respected mainstream historians on occasion, but his historical observations fall as far out of bounds of mainstream history as do theirs.[70]

Unlike Stenger and Weinberg, Michael Shermer raised doubts and questions about Dawkins's *The God Delusion* in a generally favorable review.[71] For one, he thought a more neutral title for the book would be *The God Question*. For another, he challenged Dawkins's disparaging remarks about all religious people and his dismissal of religious moderates as "enablers of terrorism." On the history front, he disagreed with the assertion that without religion there would be, in Dawkins's words, "no suicide bombers, no 9/11, no 7/7, no Crusades, no witch-hunts, no Gunpowder Plot, no Indian partition, no Israeli/Palestinian wars, no Serb/Croat massacres, no persecution of Jews as 'Christ-Killers,' no Northern Ireland 'troubles.'" In Shermer's opinion, "many of these events— and others often attributed solely to religion by atheists—were less religiously motivated than politically driven, or at the very least involved religion in the service of political hegemony." Although that eminently sensible perspective on history calls into question Dawkins's historical judgment, Shermer concludes that "*The God Delusion* deserves multiple readings, not just as an important work of science, but as a great work of literature."

Shermer's good historical sense may help us as we move toward summarizing the characteristics of misguided and misleading portrayals of the past. What, in other words, qualifies as bad history—as history outside the discipline's acceptable boundaries? We have already heard some voices on what good and bad history is all about, including J. H. Hexter, John Tosh, and Richard Evans. A helpful guide at this point is the book by Shermer and Alex Grobman, *Denying History*.[72] Shermer, founder and publisher of *Skeptic* magazine, serves as an adjunct professor of the History of Science at Occidental College. Grobman is a historian and president of the Brenn Institute, founding editor-in-chief of the *Simon Wiesenthal Annual*, and author or editor of several books on the Holocaust and modern Jewish history.

They wrote their book on Holocaust denial just as the Irving libel trial against Deborah Lipstadt got under way, but before its conclusion. The special value of *Denying History* for this book is the attention it pays to the criteria for distinguishing between legitimate and illegitimate history, or as they put it in one section, "History and Pseudohistory."[73] These criteria overlap and often coincide with the criteria applied here and will therefore help in placing New Atheist historiography somewhere on the spectrum from the best to the worst forms of presenting the past. In other words, Shermer and Grobman place Holocaust denial within the broader context of what constitutes acceptable and unacceptable methods of doing history on any and all subjects.

The purpose of their book "is to reveal the difference between history and pseudohistory by using the Holocaust denial as a classic case study in how the past may be revised for present political and ideological purposes." They realize that in an age of the "democratization of knowledge," we all may have things to say about the past, "but if we want to be taken seriously, we must obey the rules of reason and apply the tools of science and scholarship."[74] To get to those rules and tools, they give their own synopsis of modern historiography, covering much of the same ground as we did earlier in this chapter.

They discern three tiers of history in the past two centuries. They label the first *historical* objectivity, stemming from Leopold von Ranke and exemplified by J. B. Bury's already-cited comment that history is a science, "no less and no more." The second tier developed in the twentieth century as *historical relativism*, culminating in the postmodernists, who blurred the line between fact and fiction. The first tier emphasized knowable, scientifically verifiable history in the tradition of nineteenth-century positivism. The second tier presented history as existing only in the minds of historians and in the texts they produced, thus undermining our ability to know anything with certainty about the past. "Here we find a seedbed for pseudohistory and Holocaust denial."[75]

Shermer and Grobman construct a third tier, *historical science*, which reveals to us their definition of the boundaries of good and acceptable historical practice. The third tier brings us to "where all historians reside when they are truly practicing history." Key points in their version of historical science include acknowledging that "history exists both inside and outside the minds of historians." It includes recognizing that everyone, including historians, has bias and interests that shape their thinking about the past but asks only that the "quality and quantity of the bias" be evaluated, a point similar to John Tosh's admonition that historians state openly their own backgrounds, interests, and points of view. Shermer and Grobman express confidence that historians have the methods to investigate in a scientific manner the nature of historical causality.

Finally, the "historians' job is to present the past as a provisional interpretation of 'what actually happened,' based on current available evidence, much as natural scientists do with evidence from the natural world."[76]

The authors next offer a statement on Holocaust denial worthy of full quotation as a useful guide to examining any case of pseudohistory:

> The Holocaust deniers (conveniently) disregard any convergence of evidence; instead, they pick out what suits their theory and ignore the rest. They divorce their chosen details from the overall context. We contend that instead of revising history, instead of modifying a theory based on new evidence or a new interpretation of old evidence, the Holocaust deniers are engaged in pseudohistory, the rewriting of the past for present purposes. Historical revision should not be based on political ideology, religious conviction, or other human emotions. Historians are humans with emotions, of course, but if they are true revisionists, and not ideologues, they will weed out the emotional chaff from the factual wheat.[77]

By Shermer and Grobman's definition, New Atheist history qualifies as "pseudohistory." As they and other historians we have cited throughout testify, when ideologues use history for the sole purpose of furthering their ideology, they distort and manipulate history. The New Atheists and their allies view history through an ideological prism that demonizes their archenemy, religion. They pose as outsiders and victims fighting valiantly against those who threaten us with everything from a takeover of our government by the Christian right to international terrorism from Islamist extremism. The New Atheist professions of rationality and adherence to Enlightenment ideals fail to take concrete form when they present history. They need to practice what they preach and join the rest of us in trying to grasp the past for whatever help it may give us in understanding our present condition.

CHAPTER 5

What's at Stake

> One of the lessons of 9/11 is that there is no greater source of terrorism, strife, bloodshed, persecution or war than religion.
> —Full-page ad of The Freedom From Religion Foundation, *New York Times*, September 9, 2008

This book concerns the growing acceptance of the distorted understanding of the past disseminated by New Atheist historiography, illustrated in this ad from the Freedom From Religion Foundation. We began with the Big Three of Harris, Dawkins, and Hitchens, but we conclude with a wider cast that includes followers who explicitly support the Big Three, plus fellow travelers and enablers who go along directly or indirectly with the New Atheist take on history.

Science and self-professed rationality furnish the cloak that covers New Atheist pronouncements on any number of subjects. Followers make the non sequitur of believing that the New Atheist profession of scientific method gives legitimacy to their assertions of truth on matters outside the realm of science, such as history and moral progress. Consider the testimony of Christian Koeder on "what the vegan movement can learn from Richard Dawkins": "What can we learn from Dawkins? Answer: a scientific approach. This means rather than choosing a position and then defending it no matter what—using any possible argument we can find supporting it, while ignoring arguments or information that might contradict our opinion—the scientific approach means never pretending to know all the answers, not hiding information because 'it doesn't look good,' and using logic, evidence and reason to draw conclusions, not wishful thinking and blind faith. The scientific approach means looking at the evidence." Koeder then invites his readers to watch Dawkins's video on religion, "The root of all evil?"[1]

The case presented here surveys and critiques the egregious failure of Dawkins and his cohorts to abide by the rules of evidence and reasoning employed by historians trained in the methods of their craft. Christian Koeder is not alone in accepting at face value Dawkins's professions of scientific rationality while failing to notice that Dawkins's rants on religion are based largely on citation of unreliable and distorted historical evidence.

Sam Harris's *The End of Faith* got the New Atheist ball rolling. It struck a chord following September 11 in warning of the dangers of radical Islam and the political influence of right-wing American fundamentalist and evangelical Protestantism. Reviewers tended to applaud his effort, occasionally questioning his more extreme assertions. Overall, few challenged Harris or exercised skepticism toward his arguments, and virtually none commented on his abundant use of history to spell out the dangers of all religion throughout all history. His book earned him the PEN/ Martha Albrand Award given annually to the best first book in nonfiction by an American author.

Natalie Angier in *The New York Times* comments that "Harris writes what a sizable number of us think" and follows by quoting Harris's thumbnail sketch of Christianity and the danger that "allows otherwise normal human beings to reap the fruits of madness and consider them holy." She seems to go along with his attack on religious moderates as well as his search for "a mystical dimension of life . . . without recourse to superstition and credulity." After a few references to Harris's more dubious statements, she concludes, "Still, this is an important book, on a topic that, for all its inherent difficulty and divisiveness, should not be shielded from the crucible of human reason."[2]

A number of reviewers struck the same chords on tone and substance as Angier's review—general acceptance of what Harris had to stay with a few questions on some issues, followed by an overall endorsement. Stephanie Merritt in *The Observer* highlights Harris's "impassioned reappraisal of an old thesis—the idea that religion remains the primary source of human conflict," without questioning that thesis's validity. She does slap his wrist for occasionally "slipping into incredulous sarcasm." She concludes with an endorsement based on her acceptance of his central argument as sound: "Religion is the only area of human knowledge in which it is still acceptable to hold beliefs dating from antiquity and a modern society should subject those beliefs to the same principles that govern scientific, medical or geographical inquiry—particularly if they are inherently hostile to those with different ideas."[3]

When Dawkins's *The God Delusion* and Hitchens's *God Is Not Great* appeared, the fame and notoriety of the New Atheists guaranteed widespread media coverage and reviews. Religious reviewers took issue of course with the atheism but largely left the question of history out of the argument. Dawkins received somewhat harsher treatment than did Harris, even from critics who did not quarrel with his atheism. H. Allen Orr, for example, found Dawkins out of his depth "when attempting to reason philosophically." Although Orr does not delve into the historical arguments Dawkins presents, he puts his finger on the problem that has played a key role in our historical critique of New Atheists: "He has a preordained set of conclusions at which he's determined to arrive. Consequently, Dawkins uses any argument, however feeble, that seems to get him there and the merit of his various arguments appears judged largely by where they lead."[4]

Daniel Dennett took strong exception to Orr's critique of Dawkins in a letter to *The New York Review of Books*. Dennett self-identified with the New Atheists but unlike the Big Three did not delve into history for his attack on religion.[5] He charged Orr with wanting "to protect religion from the sort of unflinching scrutiny Dawkins and I (and Sam Harris and Louis Wolpert and others) are calling for." Orr responded by pointing out that he had no problem with where Dawkins arrived (his atheism) but how he got there: "It's one thing to think carefully about religion and conclude it's dubious. It's another to string together anecdotes and exercises in bad philosophy and conclude that one has resolved subtle problems. I wasn't disappointed in *The God Delusion* because I was shocked by Dawkins's atheism. I was disappointed because it wasn't very good."[6]

Terry Eagleton unloaded the strongest attack on *The God Delusion* in the pages of *The London Review of Books*. He opened with, "Imagine someone holding forth on biology whose only knowledge of the subject is the *Book of British Birds*, and you have a rough idea of what it feels like to read Richard Dawkins on theology." Eagleton continues by offering a synopsis of Christian theology aimed at revealing how crude and ill-informed Dawkins's attack on Christianity is. Along the way, he mentions a few bits of history, but that is not the focus of his review. Toward the end, he does attack Dawkins for his faith in human progress: "Dawkins... believes in his own Herbert Spencerish way, that 'the progressive trend is unmistakable and it will continue.' So there we are, then: we have it from the mouth of Mr Public Science himself that aside from a few local, temporary hiccups like ecological disasters, famine, ethnic wars and nuclear wastelands, History is perpetually on the up."[7]

Reviewers of *God Is Not Great* treated Hitchens well enough but often commented on his overzealous and overblown assertiveness that sought to bludgeon opponents. Some, like Mary Ridell, faulted Hitchens for not delving more deeply into why religion continued to attract so many adherents. Nevertheless, "Hitchens is right in much of what he says. Religion is a charter for war and human suffering." Ridell then ticks off a list of horrors perpetrated by religious fanatics.[8] Michael Kinsley likened Hitchens to an "old-fashioned village atheist, standing in the square trying to pick arguments with the good citizens on their way to church." Kinsley expresses some doubt that the logical fallacies of religion given in the book "add up to a sustained argument, because Hitchens thinks a sustained argument shouldn't even be necessary and yet wouldn't be sufficient." Kinsley applauds Hitchens erudition and concludes that *God Is Not Great* is "a serious and deeply felt book."[9]

Anthony Gottlieb offers a more probing assessment of the books by all the Big Three. He notes some of the inaccurate facts purveyed by Hitchens. Hitchens's "provocative" language elicits the observation, "It's possible to wonder, indeed, where plain speaking ends and misanthropy begins." Gottlieb does not question Hitchens's historical veracity but gives some examples of his "lopsided" evidence on the recent past: "He discussed the role of the Dutch Reformed Church in maintaining apartheid in South Africa, but does not mention the role of the Anglican Church in ending it."[10]

This sample of the Big Three's reception indicates something of the range of opinions and the controversy generated by the New Atheism. For our purposes here, it further shows a general lack of interest in the historical evidence offered in these bestselling books. In other words, Harris, Dawkins, and Hitchens got a "free pass" as historians. Books and blogs since their books appeared reveal widespread acceptance of their version of history. The evidence in this book shows that New Atheist historiography has grown, is growing, and will likely continue to grow in the immediate future.

Writers need not be committed subscribers to hard-core New Atheism to find the movement's views of the past acceptable.

Mitchell Stephens's recent book *Imagine There's No Heaven: How Atheism Helped Create the Modern World* (2014) provides an example. Stephens's history aims to show the benefits of atheism ushering in the modern world with "humankind's greatest accomplishments: the advancement of knowledge and the expansion of human rights. Subtracting the overbearing gods from the heavens encouraged the growth of learning and liberty on earth."[11] While Stephens has a few kind words to say about the influence of religion on art and occasionally morality, he bases his argument on a zero-sum game in which religion must decline and atheism advance to achieve the progress evident in the modern world. In a sense, he resuscitates a more subtle version of the "war between science and religion." It is a well-stated case charting the emergence of atheism in the past several centuries.

Although lacking hard-core New Atheist ideology, Stephens qualifies as a "fellow traveler" when it comes to general endorsements of the Big Three. He finds the books of Harris, Dawkins, and Hitchens "are powerful arguments against religion." Dawkins uses science, Hitchens "disputes religion's historical and moral claims," and Harris "underlines the connections among various contemporary outrages and religions, particularly Islam."[12]

Stephens also buys into some of the historical judgments of the New Atheists. The either/or approach, for example, works for Hitler, who believed he was an agent of Providence. Therefore he doesn't represent atheism and that is all that needs to be said. No further inquiry follows as to the sources of Hitler's beliefs.

Stephens gives a treatment of atheistic regimes—Stalin, Mao, Pol Pot, and so on—that fits snugly with Harris, Dawkins, and Hitchens. He acknowledges the persecution of believers, clergy, and the institutional church but sees it only as developing in the circumstances of the early 1920s, not as a consequence of the Marxist ideology animating Lenin, Stalin, and the Bolshevik leadership. He then chronicles the efforts of the regime to destroy religion through both persecution and persuasion. Once again he does not subject Lenin, Stalin, and the others to an analysis of their ideologies and the policies that flowed from them. His response to the charge that the "absence of religion" may have played a role in these atrocities "is the argument that, like Hébert and other members of the cult of the guillotine in 1793, Lenin, Stalin, Mao and Pol Pot *were* in a sense religious."[13]

Stephens concludes this topic with the ledger-book approach of Harris, Stenger, Avalos, and other New Atheists historians: "The similarities between the persecution of the religious in the Soviet Union and the persecution of the insufficiently religious that had been widespread throughout history was hard to miss. By the middle of the twentieth century, it would become common to label Marxism 'the god that failed.' Might we not reasonably move its brutalities and horrors from disbelief's ledger to that of the substitutes for religion?"[14] Somehow at the root of twentieth-century mass killing there lay religion or something like religion or substitutes for religion or religion look-alikes. The question of where all this "religion" came from gets left unattended, consistent with New Atheist historiography. It is not reasonable or convincing to move these atrocities to the "substitutes-for-religion" column of the ledger and walk away from the subject.

These conclusions conform to the websites that deal with historical subjects using only their own set of historical criteria about what counts and what does not. One site begins its presentation of Hitler and Stalin by declaring that "Hitler, however, was *never* an atheist" and goes on to declare that Stalin's short stay in a Russian Orthodox seminary as a teenager formed "the dogmatic black or white outlook of the world [that] influenced his subsequent actions."[15] Another begins an article with the question, "How many people in Communist Russia and China have been killed because of atheism and secularism?" The immediate conclusion is, "None, probably."[16] The main argument maintains that since atheism is the absence of belief, it doesn't lead to anything—not exactly a probing analysis of what motivated Marxist regimes. In this view of history, what we do know is that "the Catholic and Protestant Churches in Germany set the foundation of WWII and the atrocities to occur. Popes, priests and nuns supported Hitler's regime. Indeed, Hitler could not have come to power without Christianity's help."[17]

There lurks a straw man in the historical contortions of these websites and among New Atheists in general—namely, the charge that atheism always leads to immorality and evil. The New Atheists and their allies are correct in rejecting this opinion, but it is the opinion of some of their ideological opponents, not historians, including this one. It does not furnish an excuse for the systematic distortion of history by New Atheists.

Imagine There's No Heaven and similar histories signal a growing interest in assessing the role of atheism, agnosticism, and nonbelief in traditional religion in the development of modern Europe and America. In that sense, it is another example of how our contemporary interests influence what we look for in history. One of the benefits of the bestsellers by the Big Three New Atheists is the appearance of these new books giving fuller treatment of atheism historically. The hope here is that these histories can and will avoid New Atheist ideology in searching the past.

Peter Watson begins his recent book *The Age of Atheists* with Nietzsche's declaration that "God is dead" and continues for more than five hundred pages tracing, in the words of the subtitle, "How We Have Sought to Live since the Death of God." Watson's rich investigation covers a wide range of philosophical, literary, artistic, and cultural responses to that challenge.

For the most part, Watson avoids a ham-fisted attack on religion and does not chronicle the history of the evils and atrocities of religion in the manner of the New Atheists. He does manifest his opinion of religion from time to time. In commenting on recent scientific findings on religion as a natural phenomenon, he wonders, "What are we to make of this state of affairs, in which atheism has the better case, where its evidence involves new elements, which introduces new arguments, but where religion, so its adherents claim, has the numbers, despite its manifest horrors and absurdities."[18] A few pages later, he wonders how much impact his book will have "when set against the absurd, tragic and horrific dimensions of recent religious history," as he presents "an extensive survey of the work of those talented people—artists, novelists, dramatists, poets, scientists, psychologists, philosophers—who have embraced atheism, the death of God, and sought other ways to live."[19]

He begins his chapter on World War I with the declaration, "In our own day the Great War stands alongside the Holocaust, Stalin's purges, Hiroshima and Nagasaki and the Killing Fields of East Asia as one of the defining horrors of the twentieth century."[20] He offers no examination of the causes of these horrors, nor does he state that religion owned responsibility for them, but given his statement on the horrors of religion, one is left wondering if he at least implies a connection. Later in his discussion of Bertrand Russell, he quotes Russell characterizing the First World War as "wholly Christian in origin" and the dangerous features of Soviet communism as "reminiscent of the medieval Church."[21] His chapters on "The Bolshevik Crusade for Scientific Atheism" and the "Nazi Religion of the Blood" concern themselves with ideology rather than the atrocities of the regimes, although the latter are briefly described.

Watson notes the work of Harris, Dawkins, and Hitchens but does not have a lot to say about them. He does discuss Harris's *The End of Faith*, focusing on its argument that science will ultimately lead to greater moral understanding and certainty. He links Harris to the work of Matt Ridley and Steven Pinker, noting that the trio occupies some common ground on the subject of moral progress:

"For Harris, Ridley and Pinker, then, moral progress has been and is being made—it has nothing to do with religion and never has. Trade is perhaps not usually pitched against religious values as much as science has been; but the effect is much the same. Trade is a horizontal activity, carried out between people on the same level, and by definition it is a this-worldly activity. Like most other human activities, it has evolved."[22]

The Age of Atheists deserves a wide readership, but a few red flags are in order. First, by chronicling only the nonbelievers as bringing about progress, while disparaging religion and its history as "horrific," the book has a "good guys versus bad guys" quality that undermines its credibility. Second, the book seems to share, or at least go along with, the message of moral progress in the work of Harris, Ridley, and Pinker that, at the very least, is problematic among historians as a historical master narrative. Third, Watson concentrates on admittedly remarkable and creative individuals in creating modern, secular society, but he has little to say about the role of the state in that society. He notes the views of thinkers like A. C. Grayling, Jürgen Habermas, and several others on how they related politics in general to individual and community life. Yet the modernity built on the achievements of Watson's creative and innovative characters has also led to the horrors of modern warfare and genocide carried out by the secular state. Watson only notes the "infinity of horrors committed in the name of religion" that has driven people away from belief in God, while ignoring the horrors carried out by the modern state.[23]

Steven Pinker argues in *The Better Angels of Ourselves* that the development of the state has led to greater safety for greater numbers of people. Pinker has great confidence that he has the numbers to prove his case historically, although some reviewers have questioned his calculations. Our concern here has to do with his claims that science validates his views of history, recently put with great force in his article, "Science Is Not Your Enemy: A Plea for an Intellectual Truce," which he addresses "To the Neglected Novelists, Embattled English Professors, Tenure-less Historians and Other Struggling Denizens of the Humanities."

Pinker may call for a "truce," but the article has the tone of a declaration of war, combined with a declaration of the victory of science over the humanities. Here I only call into question some examples of his treatment of history. Early on he attacks Jackson Lears's article in the *Nation* reviewing three books by Sam Harris and cited in Chapter 4. He takes offense at a passage by Lears on positivism, Social Darwinism, and "pop-evolutionary notions of progress as well as scientific racism and imperialism." Lears links these ideas to the twentieth century with its two world wars and other horrors. Rather than deal with the historical argument Lears makes, Pinker simply dismisses him as a "zealous" prosecutor with a weak case: "The mindset of science cannot be blamed for genocide and war . . . It is, rather, indispensable in all areas of human concern, including politics, the arts, and the search for meaning, purpose, and morality."

Later in the article, Pinker denounces "a demonization campaign [that] anachronistically impugns science for crimes that are as old as civilization, including racism, slavery, conquest and genocide." He goes on to rail against "historically illiterate" notions that blame "science for eugenics." Again, Pinker does not engage in a historical discussion of these topics, where there is ample room for debate. He simply dismisses them as illegitimate subjects. Apparently, in his view, historians should not dare to raise questions about the possible consequences or by-products of scientific or even pseudoscientific ideas.

Pinker concludes with praise for the increasing application of science to politics. The advent of "data science" will lead to solutions in our political life. In general, the humanities should stop resisting science and get on board: "As with politics, the advent of data science applied to books, periodicals, correspondence, and musical scores holds the promise for an expansive new 'digital humanities.'"[24]

Leon Wieseltier wrote a spirited counterattack in defense of the humanities that appeared in the September 3, 2013, edition of the *New Republic*: "Crimes against Humanities: Now Science Wants to Invade the Liberal Arts. Don't Let It Happen." In his defense of the humanities, Wieseltier touches on many issues pertinent to our defense of the discipline of history. He notes, for example, "Medieval and modern religious thinking often relied upon the science of its day . . . What was Jewish and Christian and Muslim theology without Aristotle?" He goes on to emphasize the "autonomy of the humanities," as we have defended the autonomy of history. These disciplines must not fall prey to the "scientizers." He rejects Pinker's attempt to make the humanities "the handmaiden of the sciences, and dependent upon the sciences for their advance and even their survival."

Wieseltier's most fundamental point for our purposes rejects the notion that only science and its methods yield truth: "Philosophy and literature and history and critical scholarship also espouse skepticism, open debate, formal precision (though not of the mathematical kind), and—at the higher reaches of humanistic labor—even empirical tests." Finally, he accuses Pinker of showing "no trace of the skepticism whose absence he deplores in others."[25]

The same lack of skepticism manifested itself in the enthusiastic reception of the Big Three New Atheists by their supporters. In addition, no one took on their use of history with a rigorous review of their claims to historical truth. As we have seen, Michael Shermer came close in expressing some skepticism of Dawkins's historical pronouncements, but then Shermer, the founder and publisher of *Skeptic* magazine, backed off and declared *The God Delusion* a "classic." My book aims to subject the New Atheist portrayal of the past to the same rigorous review and skeptical appraisal they claim to practice and demand of everyone else.

Conclusion

The home page of the New Atheist website declares, "It is the responsibility of the educated to educate the uneducated, lest we fall prey to the tyranny of ignorance."[26] The problem with New Atheist historiography is its ignorance of history. More precisely, it is ignorance of what trained historians have researched and written on subjects New Atheists use in their relentless attack on religion and its evils throughout all history. In their zeal to make their case, they have not bothered to take advantage of the history available to them. They may fondly recall John Lennon's beautiful song "Imagine" with its opening line, "Imagine there's no heaven," but they qualify for Sam Cooke's hit, "Wonderful World," and its opening line, "Don't know much about history."

The result is a sort of pseudohistory, or what I have deemed "history out of bounds." It is not confined, of course, to the New Atheists. A broad range of examples exists today and they keep spreading, with special thanks to the Internet, which makes it easier than ever to organize and disseminate bogus ideas of all sorts. History out of bounds, with its strident insistence on a fixed and static view of the past, threatens to frustrate a broader and deeper approach to history. If we accept the idea that slavery did not have anything to do with the origins and course of the Civil War, we will never understand the nature of that greatest of all our conflicts. If we accept the idea that the United States was intentionally founded as a Christian nation, we will never understand our Founding Fathers and our Constitution. If we accept the idea that the Holocaust as commonly presented never took place, we will never understand the nature of Hitler's movement and regime and the course of World War II. If we accept the idea that religion poisoned everything in the past and that religion has been the major cause of war and death in history, we will never understand the course of history, the nature of human conflict, and the complex forces and factors that have shaped the past.

To separate legitimate history from pseudohistory, we need to alert ourselves to the characteristics that define one or the other. We look, for example, for the evidence presented and where it comes from. We take note of the tone, attitude, and vocabulary used. When we suspect that sources are weak, absent, or manipulated, we check them out. The Internet swarms with websites of bad history but also gives us quick access to sound opinions and information from mainstream historians. We have the right and obligation to become suspicious of versions of history that lack nuance and context, appearing to cherry-pick bits of information to support established positions. As we have seen, sweeping historical generalizations and simplified black-and-white presentations of the past do not characterize the work of historians.

New Atheist historians relish issuing moral judgments about the past. They do not hesitate to condemn individuals, institutions, religions, and religion in general. Their absolutist pronouncements leave no room for further discussion or broader consideration of those condemned. They further confuse us by employing a loose vocabulary in which the meaning of words becomes muddled and unclear, beginning with the one most frequently invoked: *religion*.

Particular groups or "schools" of pseudohistorians typically operate as a kind of subgroup that constantly reinforces its members' established points of view, as we have seen among the New Atheists and their supporters. The result is history by repetition rather than reason. Historical reflection cut off from mainstream historians can take on a fortress-like quality, warding off alien and unwelcome ideas. Ideological certitude combined with ignorance makes a potent cocktail of pseudotruth that easily leads to intolerance and worse.

Atheists, agnostics, theists, Christians, Jews, Muslims, those of no faith tradition, and everybody else would be well served to work within mainstream history. New Atheists, in particular, champion the use of reason and claim to stand in the tradition of the Enlightenment. Many of the rest of us value reason as well and ask only that they live up to their professed ideals when invoking the past. We invite New Atheists to apply to historical evidence the same standard Victor Stenger proclaims in interpreting evidence in general: "I must repeat what I say in all my books about interpreting evidence. A good scientist does not approach the analysis of evidence with a mind shut like a trap door against unwelcome conclusions."[27] Rational people of all persuasions have a stake in seeking together an understanding of the past, no matter how difficult and contentious that may be. The discipline of history and its practitioners provide the framework within which that can happen.

Notes

Introduction

1. Sam Harris, *The End of Faith: Religion, Terror, and the Future of Reason* (New York: W. W. Norton, 2005), 26.
2. "In New Approach, More Atheists Are Shouting It from Rooftops," *New York Times*, April 27, 2009; "Number of Groups for Atheists Skyrockets on College Campuses," *Boston Globe*, November 27, 2009. For statistics, visit the webpage of the American Religious Identification Survey (ARIS): http://www.americanreligionsurvey-aris.org. For some recent accounts of Richard Dawkins's appearances on college campuses, see articles in the *New York Times*: "An Appetite for Richard Dawkins," October 15, 2013, Portland State University, and "Famed Scientist, Author Richard Dawkins Speaks to Packed Pick-Strayer [Concert Hall]," October 4, 2103, Northwestern University.
3. J. H. Hexter, "The Historian and His Day," in *Reappraisals in History*, Second Edition (Chicago: University of Chicago Press, 1979), 8.

Chapter 1

1. Richard Dawkins, *The God Delusion* (Boston: Houghton Mifflin, 2006), 273.
2. Ibid., 249.
3. Ibid., 273.
4. Harris, *End of Faith*, 79.
5. Ibid., 231.
6. Christopher Hitchens, *God Is Not Great: How Religion Poisons Everything* (New York: Hachette, 2007), 246.
7. Ibid., 247.
8. Ibid., 248.

9. Ibid., 249.
10. Harris, *End of Faith*, 242.
11. Hitchens, *God Is Not Great*, 250.
12. Dawkins, *God Delusion*, 272ff.
13. Ibid., 278.
14. Ibid., 274.
15. John Toland, "Living History," *Journal of Historical Review* 11:1 (Spring 1991): 5–24.
16. John Toland, *Hitler* (Garden City, NY: Doubleday, 1976).
17. "John Toland," Revisionists.com, http://www.revisionists.com/revisionists/toland.html.
18. John Lukacs, *The Hitler of History* (New York: Vintage, 1997), 232. Lukacs lists a number of deficiencies in both method and substance in Toland's book, footnote pp. 22–23.
19. Of the biographies, the two volumes by Ian Kershaw stand out: *Hitler, 1889–1936: Hubris* and *Hitler, 1936–1945: Nemesis* (New York: W. W. Norton, 1999, 2000).
20. Harris, *End of Faith*, 100–107.
21. Ibid., 101.
22. Ibid., 79.
23. Ibid., 105.
24. Hitchens, *God Is Not Great*, 232.
25. Ibid., 233.
26. Ibid., 293.
27. Ibid., 241.
28. Ibid., 251.
29. Ibid., 236–51.
30. For example, Abbott Gleason, *Totalitarianism: The Inner History of the Cold War* (New York: Oxford University Press, 1995); Bruce F. Pauley, *Hitler, Stalin, and Mussolini: Totalitarianism in the Twentieth Century*, Second Edition (Wheeling, IL: Harlan Davidson, 2003); David D. Roberts, *The Totalitarian Experiment in Twentieth-Century Europe: Understanding the Poverty of Great Politics* (New York: Routledge, 2006); A. James Gregor, *Totalitarianism and Political Religion: An Intellectual History* (Stanford: Stanford University Press, 2012). Also see the pioneering study by Carl J. Friedrich and Zbigniew Brzezinski, *Totalitarian Dictatorship and Autocracy* (New York: Praeger, 1956).

Notes • 173

31. Hitchens, *God Is Not Great*, 231.
32. For a recent discussion of Arendt's book, see Michael Burleigh, *The Third Reich* (New York: Hill and Wang, 2000), 17–23.
33. Hitchens, *God Is Not Great*, 232.
34. Ibid., 251.
35. See, for example, Roger B. Beck, *The History of South Africa* (Westport, CT: Greenwood, 2000); Robert Ross, *The Concise History of South Africa* (Cambridge: Cambridge University Press, 1999); T. R. H. Davenport and Christopher Saunders, *South Africa: A Modern History*, Fifth Edition (New York: St. Martin's, 2000); Håkan Thörn, *Anti-Apartheid and the Emergence of a Global Civil Society* (New York: Palgrave Macmillan, 2006).
36. Hitchens, *God Is Not Great*, 176.
37. See Richard Evans, *The Third Reich in Power* (New York: Penguin, 2005), 250.
38. John Pollard, "Fascism and Religion," in Antonio Costa Pinto, ed., *Rethinking the Nature of Fascism, Comparative Perspectives* (New York: Palgrave Macmillan, 2011), 159.
39. Dawkins, *God Delusion*, 273.
40. Victor Stenger, *The New Atheism: Taking a Stand for Science and Reason* (Amherst, NY: Prometheus, 2009).
41. Stenger, *New Atheism*, 115.
42. Paul Froese, *The Plot to Kill God: Findings from the Soviet Experiment in Secularization* (Berkeley: University of California Press, 2008), 53.
43. Stenger, *New Atheism*, 115.
44. Ibid., 226.
45. Stenger, *New Atheism*, 116.
46. Edward Radzinsky, *Stalin: The First In-Depth Biography Based on Explosive Documents from Russia's Secret Archives* (New York: Anchor, 1997), 244–49.
47. Ibid., 249.
48. Ibid., 473.
49. Ibid., 507–8.
50. Hector Avalos, *Fighting Words: The Origins of Religious Violence* (Amherst, NY: Prometheus, 2005), 331.
51. Ibid., 330.
52. Ibid., 116.
53. Pauley, *Hitler, Stalin, and Mussolini*, 144–45.

54. Robert Service, *Stalin: A Biography* (Cambridge, MA: Belknap, 2005), 268.
55. Zoe Knox, *Russian Society and the Orthodox Church: Religion in Russia after Communism* (London: Routledge Curzon, 2005), 48.
56. See the newsletter *Freethought Today*, September 7, 2005.
57. "The renovationist movement, also known as the Living Church, divided the Russian Orthodox Church from 1922 to 1946. Renovationists attempted (unsuccessfully) to combine the beliefs of Orthodox Christianity with the political and social goals of Bolshevism. Renovationism also allowed the remarriage of parish clergy and the marriage of bishops, both of which were forbidden by traditional Orthodox canons. Metropolitan Alexander Vvedenskii led the schism for five years until 1946." Tatiana A. Chumachenko, *Church and State in Soviet Russia: Russian Orthodoxy from World War II to the Khrushchev Years* (Armonk, NY: M. E. Sharpe, 2002), 37.
58. Avalos, *Fighting Words*, 330.
59. For numerous examples, see Orlando Figes, *The Whisperers: Private Life in Stalin's Russia* (New York: Metropolitan, 2007).
60. Knox, *Russian Society and the Orthodox Church*, 47.
61. Stenger, *New Atheism*, 114.
62. Avalos, *Fighting Words*, 304.
63. For example, see Michael Burleigh and Wolfgang Wipperman, "Racial-Hygienic Theories," in *The Racial State: Germany 1933–1945* (Cambridge: Cambridge University Press, 1991), 28–43.
64. Evans, *Third Reich in Power*, 707.
65. Richard Weikart, *From Darwin to Hitler: Evolutionary Ethics, Eugenics, and Racism in Germany* (New York: Palgrave Macmillan, 2004), 214. See also Weikart, *Hitler's Ethic: The Nazi Pursuit of Evolutionary Progress* (New York: Palgrave Macmillan, 2009); Sheila Faith Weiss, *The Nazi Symbiosis: Human Genetics and Politics in the Third Reich* (Chicago: University of Chicago Press, 2010).
66. Hector Avalos, "Atheism Was Not the Cause of the Holocaust," in John W. Loftus, ed., *The Christian Delusion: Why Faith Fails* (Amherst, NY: Prometheus, 2010), 368–95.
67. Review by John Jovan Markovic in *Journal of Church and State* 45:3 (Summer 2003): 591–92.
68. Chumachenko, *Church and State in Soviet Russia*, 187, 192. Chumachenko adds, "Between 1960 and 1964, the number of churches and

chapels decreased by 5,457 (on January 1, 1960, there were 13,008; on January 1, 1965—7,873). Eight theological seminaries were open on January 1, 1960; five of them had been closed by 1964 . . . By the mid-1960s, the Russian Orthodox Church had only 18 functioning monasteries in the USSR (on January 1, 1959, that number stood at 63, on January 1, 1960, it was 44). Those closed included the Monastery of the Caves in Kiev, the most ancient of sacred places in the Russian Orthodox Church" (187–88).
69. Evans, "Converting the Soul," in *The Third Reich in Power*, 219–320.
70. Ibid., 260.
71. John Tosh, *The Pursuit of History: Aims, Methods and New Directions in the Study of Modern History*, Revised Third Edition (London: Longman, 2002), 208.
72. Timothy Snyder, *Bloodlands: Europe between Hitler and Stalin* (New York: Basic, 2010), 400.

Chapter 2

1. Hitchens, *God Is Not Great*, 283.
2. Mona Ozouf, *Festivals of the French Revolution* (Cambridge, MA: Harvard University Press, 1991), 108.
3. Hitchens, *God Is Not Great*, 283.
4. Dawkins, *God Delusion*, 271.
5. Hitchens, *God Is Not Great*, 176. (Also chapter 1, note 34.)
6. Dawkins, *God Delusion*, 271–72.
7. Harris, *End of Faith*, 25.
8. Ibid., 63.
9. Ibid., 95–96.
10. Ibid., 257.
11. Dawkins, *God Delusion*, 103–4.
12. Hitchens, *God Is Not Great*, 211.
13. Harris, *End of Faith*, 45.
14. Ibid., 46.
15. Ibid., 243 n. 22.
16. Ibid., 88–89.
17. Ibid., 92.
18. Ibid., 85.
19. Ibid., 86.

20. Ibid., 85–86.
21. Ibid., 251, 277.
22. Ibid., 171–73. See also his endnote on free will, 272–74.
23. Ibid., 257 n. 35.
24. Ibid., 37–38.
25. Dawkins, *God Delusion*, 276.
26. Ibid., 157.
27. Ibid., 49–50.
28. Ibid., 97–99.
29. Ibid., 48.
30. Hitchens, *God Is Not Great*, 266–70.
31. Ibid., 268.
32. Ibid., 268–69.
33. Dawkins, *God Delusion*, 39.
34. Ibid., 40–41.
35. Ibid., 43.
36. Harris, *End of Faith*, 154–69.
37. Ibid., 163.
38. Ibid., 168.
39. Ibid., 144.
40. Ibid., 106.
41. Dawkins, *God Delusion*, 88, 278.
42. Ibid., 229–30, 256, 302.
43. Hitchens, *God Is Not Great*, 96.
44. For example, see Donald L. Drakeman, *Church, State, and Original Intent* (Cambridge: Cambridge University Press, 2010), 79–80.
45. R. R. Palmer, *The Age of the Democratic Revolution: A Political History of Europe and America, 1760–1800*, 2 vols. (Princeton: Princeton University Press, 1959–64).
46. Adam Frank, *Constant Fire: Beyond the Science vs. Religion Debate* (Berkeley: University of California Press, 2010), 30–31.
47. Stenger, *New Atheism*, 73–74.
48. William R. Shea, "Assessing the Relation between Science and Religion," *Historically Speaking* 7:2 (November/December 2005): 6.
49. Michael Ruse and David Hull, eds., *The Philosophy of Biology* (New York: Oxford University Press, 1998), 671.
50. Steven Shapin, *The Scientific Revolution* (Chicago: University of Chicago Press), 135–36.

51. Dawkins, *God Delusion*, 271.
52. John Lukacs, *The Future of History* (New Haven: Yale University Press, 2011), 102.
53. Sam Harris, *The Moral Landscape: How Science Can Determine Human Values* (New York: Free Press, 2010).
54. H. Allen Orr, "The Science of Right and Wrong," *New York Review of Books*, May 12, 2011.
55. Dawkins, *God Delusion*, 266.
56. Ibid., 271.
57. "Marilynne Robinson on Dawkins," Darwiniana, October 23, 2006, http://darwiniana.com/2006/10/23/marilynne-robinson-on-dawkins.
58. David Cannadine, *The Undivided Past: Humanity beyond Our Differences* (New York: Alfred A. Knopf, 2013), 43.
59. Dawkins, *God Delusion*, 278.
60. Stenger, *New Atheism*, 242.
61. Michael Burleigh, *Earthly Powers: The Clash of Religion and Politics in Europe from the French Revolution to the Great War* (New York: HarperCollins), 101.
62. Ibid., 327–34.
63. Mark Gilderhus, *History and Historians: A Historiographical Introduction*, Fifth Edition (Upper Saddle River, NJ: Prentice Hall, 2003), 80.

Chapter 3

1. Victor Stenger, *God and the Folly of Faith: The Incompatibility of Science and Religion* (Amherst, NY: Prometheus, 2012), 254–55.
2. Hitchens, *God Is Not Great*, 64.
3. Charles Freeman, *The Closing of the Western Mind: The Rise of Faith and the Fall of Reason* (New York: Vintage, 2002), xvii–xviii.
4. Ibid., xix.
5. Ibid., 4.
6. Ibid., 6.
7. William Manchester, *A World Lit Only by Fire: The Medieval Mind and the Renaissance, Portrait of an Age* (Boston: Little, Brown, 1992), xv–xvi.
8. Ibid., 293–302.
9. Ibid., 27.

10. Alex Rosenberg, *The Atheist's Guide to Reality: Enjoying Life without Illusions* (New York: Norton, 2011), 257.
11. Philip Kitcher, "Seeing Is Unbelieving," *New York Times Sunday Book Review*, March 23, 2012.
12. Will Durant, *The Age of Faith* (New York: Simon and Schuster, 1944), 1084.
13. Jeremy du Quesnay Adams, Review of *A World Lit Only by Fire*, *Speculum: The Journal of the Medieval Academy of America* 70:1 (January 1995): 173–74.
14. *Kirkus Reviews*, March 15, 1992 (review posted online May 20, 2010), https://www.kirkusreviews.com/book-reviews/william-manchester.
15. Dawkins, *God Delusion*, 252.
16. Harris, *End of Faith*, 254–55.
17. Ibid., 153.
18. Ibid., 83–84.
19. Ibid., 85.
20. Stenger, *New Atheism*, 112.
21. Stenger, *God and the Folly of Faith*, 254–55.
22. Harris, *End of Faith*, 82–107.
23. Ibid., 106.
24. Ibid., 22.
25. Ibid., 70–71.
26. Ibid., 111.
27. Ibid., 132.
28. Hitchens, *God Is Not Great*, 34, 69.
29. Harris, *End of Faith*, 254.
30. Hitchens, *God Is Not Great*, 180.
31. Quoted in Dawkins, *God Delusion*, 190.
32. Ibid., 275.
33. Hitchens, *God Is Not Great*, 233–34.
34. Ibid., 275.
35. Sam Harris, *Letter to a Christian Nation* (New York: Vintage, 2008), 12.
36. Ibid., 117.
37. Manchester, *World Lit Only by Fire*, 190.
38. Quoted in Harris, *End of Faith*, 86.
39. Manchester, *World Lit Only by Fire*, 186.
40. Ibid., 178.
41. Harris, *End of Faith*, 109.

42. C. Warren Hollister, *Medieval Europe: A Short History*, Sixth Edition (New York: McGraw-Hill, 1990), 178.
43. Paul Johnson, *A History of Christianity* (New York: Atheneum, 1980), 245.
44. Hitchens, *God Is Not Great*, 69.
45. For example, see Richard S. Dunn, *The Age of Religious Wars, 1559–1715*, Second Edition (New York: W. W. Norton, 1979).
46. For example, see the pioneering work of Lyn White Jr., *Medieval Technology and Social Change* (Oxford: Clarendon, 1962); and more recently Alfred Crosby, *The Measure of Reality: Quantification in Western Europe, 1250–1600* (Cambridge: Cambridge University Press, 1997).
47. Hitchens, *God Is Not Great*, 68.
48. Richard Carrier, "Christianity Was Not Responsible for Modern Science," in John W. Loftus, ed., *The Christian Delusion* (Amherst, NY: Prometheus, 2009), 414. For a more balanced New Atheist view, see chapter 3, "The Rebirth and Triumph of Science," in Stenger, *God and the Folly of Faith*, although he concludes the chapter quoting with approval the same passage from Carrier, "Christianity Was Not Responsible for Modern Science," 99.
49. Harris, *End of Faith*, 153.
50. Stenger, *New Atheism*, 114–15.
51. Hollister, *Medieval Europe*, 228.
52. Dawkins, *God Delusion*, 275.
53. Gleason, *Totalitarianism*, 158–59.
54. Robert Daniels, *Russia: The Roots of Confrontation* (Cambridge, MA: Harvard University Press, 1985), 170–71.
55. For example, Henry Kamen, *The Spanish Inquisition: A Historical Revision* (New Haven: Yale University Press, 1999); Edward Peters, *Inquisition* (Berkeley: University of California Press, 1989).
56. Stenger, *New Atheism*, 112–16.
57. Ibid., 115, 132 n. 17.
58. Dunn, *Age of Religious Wars*, 297.

Chapter 4

1. Harris, *End of Faith*, 16.
2. Deborah Lipstadt, *Denying the Holocaust: The Growing Assault on Truth and Memory* (New York: Free Press, 1993), 181.

3. Richard J. Evans, *Lying about Hitler* (New York: Basic, 2002).
4. Ibid., 184.
5. "Critic of a Holocaust Denier Is Cleared in British Court," *New York Times*, April 11, 2000.
6. Evans, *Lying about Hitler*, 228.
7. Gilderhus, *History and Historians*, 17.
8. Ibid., 19.
9. Ibid., 23.
10. Tosh, *Pursuit of History*, 20.
11. Gilderhus, *History and Historians*, 39.
12. L. P. Hartley as quoted in David Lowenthal, *The Past Is a Foreign Country* (Cambridge: Cambridge University Press, 1985), xvi.
13. Tosh, *Pursuit of History*, 7–8.
14. Fritz Stern, ed., *The Varieties of History: From Voltaire to the Present* (New York: Vintage, 1973), 223.
15. Tosh, *Pursuit of History*, 166.
16. Gilderhus, *History and Historians*, 76.
17. Tosh, *Pursuit of History*, 102.
18. Gilderhus, *History and Historians*, 60–61.
19. Ibid., 63.
20. Isaiah Berlin, *The Hedgehog and the Fox* (Princeton: Princeton University Press, 1953). Widely available in subsequent editions and collections of Berlin's essays.
21. Tosh, *Pursuit of History*, 186.
22. Ibid., 104.
23. Ibid., 196.
24. Ibid., 199–200.
25. For a fuller critique of postmodernism, see Richard J. Evans, *In Defense of History* (New York: W. W. Norton, 1997).
26. Dawkins, *God Delusion*, 249.
27. Ibid., 272–78.
28. Ibid., 278.
29. Anne Nicol Gaylor, "Hitler's Religion," Freedom From Religion Foundation, http://ffrf.org/publications/freethought-today/articles/hitlers-religion.
30. John Glover, *Humanity: A Moral History of the 20th Century*, Second Edition (New Haven: Yale University Press, 2000).
31. Harris, *End of Faith*, 79, 252 n. 36.

32. Glover, *Humanity*, 310–11.
33. Ibid., 356.
34. Ibid., 317.
35. Ibid., 405.
36. Richard Carrier, "'Hitler's Table Talk' Troubling Finds," *German Studies Review* 26:31 (October 2003): 561–76. A slightly different version appeared in *Freethought Today* 19:9 (November 2002), published by the Freedom From Religion Foundation.
37. Richard Carrier, *Not the Impossible Faith: Why Christianity Didn't Need a Miracle to Succeed* (Raleigh, NC: Lulu, 2009).
38. Bart Ehrman, *Did Jesus Exist? The Historical Argument for Jesus of Nazareth* (New York: HarperCollins, 2012), 296.
39. Richard Carrier, "Ehrman on Jesus: A Failure of Facts and Logic," FreethoughtBlogs, April 19, 2012, http//freethoughtblogs.com/carrier/archives/1026.
40. Dawkins, *God Delusion*, 97; Hitchens, *God Is Not Great*, 114.
41. Bart Ehrman, "Fuller Reply to Richard Carrier," Bart Ehrman Blog, April 25, 2012, http://ehrmanblog.org/fuller-reply-to-richard-carrier.
42. The endnotes are found in Dawkins, *God Delusion*, 395.
43. Alan Bullock, *Hitler and Stalin: Parallel Lives* (New York: Vintage, 1993), 381.
44. Daniel Goldhagen, *Hitler's Willing Executioners: Ordinary Germans and the Holocaust* (New York: Alfred A. Knopf, 1996).
45. Harris, *End of Faith*, 99–100.
46. Ron Rosenbaum, *Explaining Hitler: The Search for the Origins of Evil* (New York: Random House, 1998), 346. For Rosenbaum's full discussion of the Goldhagen controversy, see chapter 19, "Daniel Goldhagen: Blaming Germans," 337–68. Harris lists Rosenbaum's book in his bibliography.
47. Raul Hilberg, "The Goldhagen Phenomenon," *Critical Inquiry* 23 (Summer 1997): 728.
48. Ruth Bettina Birn, "Revising the Holocaust," *The Historical Journal* 40:1 (1997): 215.
49. Omar Bartov, "Ordinary Monsters," *New Republic*, April 29, 1996.
50. Jonathan Riley-Smith, *The Crusades: A History* (New Haven: Yale University Press, 2005); Thomas Madden, *The New Concise History of the Crusades* (Lanham, MD: Rowman and Littlefield, 2005); Thomas Asbudge, *The First Crusade* (New York: Free Press, 2004);

Erik Middlefort, *Witch Hunting in Southwestern Germany, 1562–1684: The Social and Intellectual Foundations* (Stanford: Stanford University Press, 1972); Brian Levack, *The Witch Hunt in Early Modern Europe* (New York: Routledge, 2013).
51. In Loftus, *Christian Delusion*, 414.
52. For example, see David J. Mattingly, *Imperialism, Power, and Identity: Experiencing the Roman Empire* (Princeton: Princeton University Press, 2012); Peter Brown, "Paganism: What We Owe the Christians," review of Alec Cameron, *The Last Pagans of Rome*, *New York Review of Books*, April 11, 2011.
53. Jackson Lears, "Same Old New Atheism: On Sam Harris," *Nation*, April 27, 2011.
54. Harris, *End of Faith*, 16.
55. Steven Pinker, "Science Is Not Your Enemy," *New Republic*, August 19, 2013.
56. Steven Pinker, *The Better Angels of Our Nature: Why Violence Has Declined* (New York: Viking, 2012).
57. For a spirited rebuttal of Pinker's article, see Leon Wieseltier, "Crimes against Humanities, Now Science Wants to Invade the Liberal Arts. Don't Let It Happen," *New Republic*, September 3, 2013.
58. For example, Christopher Hitchens, "Defending Islamofascism, It's a Valid Term. Here's Why," *Slate*, October 22, 2007.
59. Chris Hedges, *When Atheism Becomes Religion* (New York: Free Press, 2008), 140–41. Previously published in hardback as *I Don't Believe in Atheists*.
60. Steven Weinberg, "Without God," *New York Review of Books*, November 20, 2008.
61. Dawkins, *God Delusion*, 249.
62. Glover, *Humanity*, 401.
63. Vincent Bugliosi, *Divinity of Doubt: The God Question* (New York: Viking, 2011).
64. Ibid., 229.
65. Ibid., 163, 223–24.
66. Ibid., 162, 228.
67. Ibid., 228–29.
68. Service, *Stalin*, 301.
69. Knox, *Russian Society and the Orthodox Church*, 45.
70. Bugliosi, *Divinity of Doubt*, 228–29. The other two books he references are Adam Ulam, *Stalin: The Man and His Era* (New York:

Viking, 1973); and Simon Montefiore, *Stalin: The Court of the Red Tsar* (New York: Random House, 2007). The views of these two historians are consistent with those of Robert Service, not Bugliosi.
71. Michael Shermer, review of *The God Delusion*, *Science*, June 26, 2007; see also Shermer's webpage.
72. Michael Shermer and Alex Grobman, *Denying History: Who Says the Holocaust Never Happened and Why Do They Say It?* (Berkeley: University of California Press, 2000).
73. Ibid., 1–8.
74. Ibid., 2, 5.
75. Ibid., 27.
76. Ibid., 30.
77. Ibid., 34.

Chapter 5

1. Christian Koeder, April 14, 2014, http://www.christiankoeder.com.
2. Natalie Angier, "'The End of Faith': Against Toleration," *New York Times*, September 5, 2004.
3. Stephanie Merritt, "Faith No More," *Observer Book Review*, February 6, 2005.
4. H. Allen Orr, "A Mission to Convert," *New York Review of Books*, January 11, 2007.
5. Daniel C. Dennett, *Breaking the Spell: Religion as a Natural Phenomenon* (New York: Viking, 2006).
6. "The God Delusion," Letters, *New York Review of Books*, March 1, 2007.
7. Terry Eagleton, "Lunging, Flailing, Mispunching," *London Review of Books*, October 19, 2006.
8. Mary Riddell, "The Gospel According to Hitch," *Guardian*, June 3, 2007.
9. Michael Kinsley, "In God, Distrust," Sunday Book Review, *New York Times*, May 13, 2007.
10. Anthony Gottlieb, "Atheists with Attitude: Why Do They Hate Him?" *New Yorker*, May 21, 2007.
11. Mitchell Stephens, *Imagine There's No Heaven: How Atheism Helped Create the Modern World* (New York: Palgrave Macmillan, 2014), 2.
12. Ibid., 269.
13. Ibid., 221.

14. Ibid., 223.
15. "Hitler, Stalin and Atheism," *The Rejection of Pascal's Wager*, http://www.geocites.com/paulntobin/hitlerstalin.html.
16. Austin Cline, "How Many Were Killed by Communists in the Name of Atheism & Secularism?" About.com, http://atheism.about.com/od/isatheismdangerous/a/AtheismKilled.htm.
17. Jim Walker, "Hitler's Christianity," NoBeliefs.com, http://www.nobeliefs.com/Hitler1.htm.
18. Peter Watson, *The Age of Atheists: How We Have Sought to Live Since the Death of God* (New York: Simon and Schuster, 2014), 11.
19. Ibid., 21–22.
20. Ibid., 187.
21. Ibid., 307.
22. Ibid., 477.
23. Ibid., 532.
24. Steven Pinker, "Science Is Not Your Enemy," *New Republic*, August 19, 2013.
25. Leon Wieseltier, "Crimes against Humanities," *New Republic*, September 3, 2013.
26. http://newatheists.org.
27. Stenger, *New Atheism*, 15.

Bibliography

Avalos, Hector. *Fighting Words: The Origins of Religious Violence* (Amherst, NY: Prometheus, 2005).

Bartov, Omar. "Ordinary Monsters," *New Republic*, April 29, 1996.

Bugliosi, Vincent. *Divinity of Doubt: The God Question* (New York: Viking, 2011).

Bullock, Alan. *Hitler and Stalin: Parallel Lives* (New York: Vintage, 1993).

Burleigh, Michael. *Earthly Powers: The Clash of Religion and Politics in Europe from the French Revolution to the Great War* (New York: HarperCollins, 2005).

———. *The Third Reich: A New History* (New York: Hill and Wang, 2000).

Burleigh, Michael, and Wolfgang Wipperman. *The Racial State: Germany 1933–1945* (Cambridge: Cambridge University Press, 1991).

Carrier, Richard. "'Hitler's Table Talk' Troubling Finds," *German Studies Review* 26:3 (October 2003): 561–76.

———. *Not the Impossible Faith: Why Christianity Didn't Need a Miracle to Succeed* (Raleigh, NC: Lulu, 2009).

Chumachenko, Tatiana A. *Church and State in Soviet Russia: Russian Orthodoxy from World War II to the Khrushchev Years* (Armonk, NY: M. E. Sharpe, 2002).

Daniels, Robert. *Russia: The Roots of Confrontation* (Cambridge, MA: Harvard University Press, 1985).

Dawkins, Richard. *The God Delusion* (Boston: Houghton Mifflin, 2006).

Dunn, Richard S. *The Age of Religious Wars, 1559–1715*, Second Edition (New York: W. W. Norton, 1979).

Ehrman, Bart. *Did Jesus Exist? The Historical Argument for Jesus of Nazareth* (New York: HarperCollins, 2012).

Evans, Richard J. *In Defense of History* (New York: W. W. Norton, 1997).

———. *Lying about Hitler: History, Holocaust, and the David Irving Trial* (New York: Basic, 2001).

———. *The Third Reich in Power* (New York: Penguin, 2005).
Figes, Orlando. *The Whisperers: Private Life in Stalin's Russia* (New York: Metropolitan, 2007).
Frank, Adam. *Constant Fire: Beyond the Science vs. Religion Debate* (Berkeley: University of California Press, 2010).
Freeman, Charles. *The Closing of the Western Mind: The Rise of Faith and the Fall of Reason* (New York: Vintage, 2002).
Froese, Paul. *The Plot to Kill God: Findings from the Soviet Experiment in Secularization* (Berkeley: University of California Press, 2008).
Gilderhus, Mark. *History and Historians: A Historiographical Introduction*, Fifth Edition (Upper Saddle River, NJ: Prentice Hall, 2003).
Gleason, Abbott. *Totalitarianism: The Inner History of the Cold War* (New York: Oxford University Press, 1995).
Glover, John. *Humanity: A Moral History of the 20th Century*, Second Edition (New Haven: Yale University Press, 2000).
Goldhagen, Daniel. *Hitler's Willing Executioners: Ordinary Germans and the Holocaust* (New York: Alfred A. Knopf, 1996).
Harris, Sam. *The End of Faith: Terror and the Future of Reason* (New York: W. W. Norton, 2005).
———. *Letter to a Christian Nation* (New York: Vintage, 2008).
———. *The Moral Landscape: How Science Can Determine Human Values* (New York: Free Press, 2010).
Hedges, Chris. *When Atheism Becomes Religion* (New York: Free Press, 2008). Previously published in hard back as *I Don't Believe in Atheists*.
Hexter, J. H. *Reappraisals in History*, Second Edition (Chicago: University of Chicago Press, 1979).
Hitchens, Christopher. *God Is Not Great: How Religion Poisons Everything* (New York: Hachette, 2007).
Hollister, C. Warren. *Medieval Europe: A Short History*, Sixth Edition (New York: McGraw-Hill, 1990).
Johnson, Paul. *A History of Christianity* (New York: Atheneum, 1980).
Kershaw, Ian. *Hitler, 1889–1936: Hubris* (New York: W. W. Norton, 1999).
———. *Hitler, 1936–1945: Nemesis* (New York: W. W. Norton, 2000).
Knox, Zoe. *Russian Society and the Orthodox Church: Religion in Russia after Communism* (London: Routledge Curzon, 2005).
Lears, Jackson. "Same Old New Atheism: On Sam Harris," *Nation*, April 27, 2011.

Lipstadt, Deborah. *Denying the Holocaust: The Growing Assault on Truth and Memory* (New York: Free Press, 1993).
Loftus, John W., ed. *The Christian Delusion: Why Faith Fails* (Amherst, NY: Prometheus, 2010).
Lukacs, John. *The Future of History* (New Haven: Yale University Press, 2011).
———. *The Hitler of History* (New York: Vintage, 1997).
Manchester, William. *A World Lit Only by Fire: The Medieval Mind and the Renaissance, Portrait of an Age* (Boston: Little, Brown, 1992).
Ozouf, Mona. *Festivals of the French Revolution* (Cambridge, MA: Harvard University Press, 1991).
Painter, Borden. "Letters," Exchange between Richard Carrier and Borden Painter, *Historically Speaking: The Bulletin of the Historical Society* 14:2 (April 2013): 34–35.
———. "New Atheism's Old—and Flawed—History," *Historically Speaking: The Bulletin of the Historical Society* 13:5 (November 2012): 15–17.
Palmer, R. R. *The Age of the Democratic Revolution: A Political History of Europe and America, 1760–1800*, 2 vols. (Princeton: Princeton University Press, 1959–64).
Pauley, Bruce F. *Hitler, Stalin, and Mussolini: Totalitarianism in the Twentieth Century*, Second Edition (Wheeling, IL: Harlan Davidson, 2003).
Pinker, Steven. *The Better Angels of Our Nature: Why Violence Has Declined* (New York: Viking, 2012).
———. "Science Is Not Your Enemy," *New Republic*, August 19, 2013.
Pollard, John. "Fascism and Religion," in Antonio Costa Pinto, ed., *Rethinking the Nature of Fascism: Comparative Perspectives* (New York: Palgrave Macmillan, 2011).
Radzinsky, Edward. *Stalin: The First In-Depth Biography Based on Explosive Documents from Russia's Secret Archives* (New York: Anchor, 1997).
Rosenbaum, Ron. *Explaining Hitler: The Search for the Origins of Evil* (New York: Random House, 1998).
Rosenberg, Alex. *The Atheist's Guide to Reality: Enjoying Life without Illusions* (New York: W. W. Norton, 2011).
Service, Robert. *Stalin: A Biography* (Cambridge, MA: Belknap, 2005).
Shapin, Steven. *The Scientific Revolution* (Chicago: University of Chicago Press, 1996).
Shea, William R. "Assessing the Relation between Science and Religion," *Historically Speaking* 7:2 (November/December 2005): 6.

Shermer, Michael. "Review, Richard Dawkins, *The God Delusion*," *Science*, June 26, 2007.

Shermer, Michael, and Alex Grobman. *Denying History: Who Says the Holocaust Never Happened and Why Do They Say It?* (Berkeley: University of California Press, 2000).

Snyder, Timothy. *Bloodlands: Europe between Hitler and Stalin* (New York: Basic, 2010).

Stenger, Victor. *God and the Folly of Faith: The Incompatibility of Science and Religion* (Amherst, NY: Prometheus, 2012).

———. *The New Atheism: Taking a Stand for Science and Reason* (Amherst, NY: Prometheus, 2009).

Stephens, Mitchell. *Imagine There's No Heaven: How Atheism Helped Create the Modern World* (New York: Palgrave Macmillan, 2014).

Stern, Fritz, ed. *The Varieties of History: From Voltaire to the Present* (New York: Vintage, 1973).

Toland, John. *Hitler* (Garden City, NY: Doubleday, 1976).

Tosh, John. *The Pursuit of History: Aims, Methods and New Directions in the Study of Modern History*, Revised Third Edition (London: Longman, 2002).

Watson, Peter. *The Age of Atheists: How We Have Sought to Live since the Death of God* (New York: Simon and Schuster, 2014).

Weikert, Richard. *From Darwin to Hitler: Evolutionary Ethics, Eugenics, and Racism in Germany* (New York: Palgrave Macmillan, 2004).

———. *Hitler's Ethic: The Nazi Pursuit of Evolutionary Progress* (New York: Palgrave Macmillan, 2009).

Weiss, Sheila Faith. *The Nazi Symbiosis: Human Genetics and Politics in the Third Reich* (Chicago: University of Chicago Press, 2010).

Index

Adams, Jeremy du Quesnay, 84
Adams, John, 55, 61
Age of Religious Wars, 72, 103
Albania, 14
Albigensians, 85, 96, 128; Albigensian Crusade, 96, 111
Angier, Natalie, 156–57
Anglicanism, 22, 159. *See also* Church of England
Annales school of history, 127
anti-Semitism, 19, 21, 37, 39, 83, 138–39, 141
Aquinas, Thomas, 81, 98, 105–6
Arendt, Hannah, 21
Augustine of Hippo, 85, 105, 121
Auschwitz, 13, 19, 56
Avalos, Hector, 2, 36–38, 40, 41, 161; *Fighting Words*, 35

Bartov, Omer, 139–40
Bayle, Peter, 142
Beck, Glenn, 3
Becket, Thomas, 77–78, 97
Benedict, Benedictine, 92–93, 97
Bentham, Jeremy, 52, 70
Berlin, Isaiah, 129, 131
Bernal, J. D., 15
bin Laden, Osama, 88
Birn, Ruth Bettin, 139
Bismarck, Otto von, 74
Black Death, 87
Bloch, Marc, 127
Boccaccio, Giovanni, 108
Bonhoeffer, Dietrich, 20, 26
Brezhnev, Leonid, 33

Bugliosi, Vincent: *Divinity of Doubt*, 149–51
Bullock, Alan, 18, 137–38; *Hitler and Stalin*, 137
Bury, J. B., 125, 153

Calvin, John, 5, 20, 21, 66, 88, 109
Calvinism, 88, 90, 102, 103. *See also* Huguenots; Puritans
Cambodia, 73, 141
Cannadine, David, 72
Carrier, Richard, 2, 135–37, 143
Castro, Fidel, 14
Cathars. *See* Albigensians
Catholicism, 19, 36, 60, 63, 64, 72, 90, 91, 102, 103, 105, 150; and the Enlightenment, 48, 61; and the French Revolution, 62, 73; and Germany, 20, 74, 162; and Hitler, 16, 18, 20, 27, 38, 133, 134, 162; and the Holocaust, 28; and Italy, 24; and the modern state, 57, 102; and Thirty Years War, 58, 103. *See also* papacy
Charlemagne, 93, 107
Charles V. *See under* Holy Roman Empire
Christianity, 5, 18, 31, 36, 53, 56, 63, 85, 86, 92, 93, 103, 109, 149, 151, 156, 158; and Anti-Semitism, 19, 138; Christian Humanists, 122; and Enlightenment, 60, 61, 80, 123; History of, 2, 4, 12, 47, 65, 79, 81, 83, 87, 91, 104; and Hitler, 16, 20, 134–35, 162; and Martin Luther King, 22, 48; and Science, 68, 98, 106, 143; and Stalin, 10

Christian Right, 5, 156
Chumachenko, Tatiana A.: *Church and State in Soviet Russia*, 40
Church of England, 20, 90, 102
Civil War, American (1861–65), 65, 74, 142, 144
communism, 5, 14, 26, 49, 52, 53, 63, 125, 134, 141, 150, 163
Comte, August, 49, 52, 53, 63, 125
Congress of Vienna, 62
Constantine, 83, 85, 92, 131
Constantinople, 92, 96, 122, 123
Copernicus, Nicholas, 60, 66, 81, 106
Cornwell, John: *Hitler's Pope*, 20
Council of Nicaea, 79
Council of Trent, 102, 105
Counter-Reformation, 89
Croce, Benedetto, 112
Crusades, 77, 83, 86, 91, 95, 96, 110, 111, 143, 150, 151

Daniels, Robert: *Russia*, 110
Dante Alighieri, 108
Dark Ages. *See* Middle Ages
Darwin, Charles, 52, 53, 54, 63
Darwinism, 66. *See also* Social Darwinism
Dawkins, Richard, 13, 15, 17, 18, 23, 47, 50, 54, 55, 57, 58, 67, 109, 133, 136, 144, 146–48, 155–56, 159, 163; and atheism, 2, 6, 9–10, 11, 16, 32, 131–32, 149, 157–58; *The God Delusion*, 1, 72, 80, 131, 148, 151–52, 157, 158, 166; as historian, 11, 31, 33, 41, 43, 53, 72, 131, 133, 142; on Hitler, 11, 16–18, 108, 132–33, 137–38, 160; on Islam, 146–47; on moral *Zeitgeist*, 48–49, 69–70, 71; on Stalin, 9, 10–11, 16, 32, 35, 36
Dennett, Daniel, 158
Descartes, Rene, 19, 60
Dominic, Dominicans, 85, 97, 98, 106
Draper, William: *History of the Conflict between Religion and Science*, 66–68
Dreyfus affair, 21

Durant, Will, 51, 82, 83–84, 88
Dutch Reformed Church, 22, 159

Eagleton, Terry, 158
Edict of Nantes, 103
Ehrman, Bart, 136–37
Einstein, Albert, 54
England: Civil War (1640s), 77, 86; Edward I, 67; Edward III, 107; Elizabeth I, 90, 102; and the Enlightenment, 3, 6, 7, 42, 45–49, 53–54, 57, 60, 61, 65, 67, 69, 70, 80, 90, 94, 112, 119, 122–23, 130–32, 134, 142–43, 145, 150, 153, 169; Glorious Revolution (1688–89), 58, 60; Henry II, 77–78, 95; Henry VIII, 78, 90, 102
Erasmus of Rotterdam, 89, 101, 122
Erikson, Eric, 126
eugenics, 15, 27, 39, 40, 141, 144–45, 164
Evans, Richard, 39, 41, 118; *Lying about Hitler*, 117–18, 152; *The Third Reich in Power*, 39

Faraday, Michael, 52
fascism, 14, 23–24, 27, 30, 117, 146
Fourth Lateran Council, 85
France, 24, 27, 46, 52, 58–60, 62, 64, 65, 73, 78, 85, 90, 96, 97, 102, 103, 107, 108, 111, 121, 128; Francis I, 103; French Revolution, 46, 62, 110, 125, 142; Henry IV, 103; Louis XIV, 58, 59, 74, 103, 122; Napoleon, 46, 62, 64, 74; Philip II, 107
Francis of Assisi, Franciscans, 87, 98, 106
Franco, Francisco, 29
Frank, Adam: *The Constant Fire*, 66
Franklin, Benjamin, 54, 55, 142
Frederick I, Frederick II. *See under* Holy Roman Empire
Freedom From Religion Foundation, 2, 18, 36, 133, 155

Freeman, Charles, 80, 143; *Closing the Western Mind*, 80
Froese, Paul: *The Plot to Kill God*, 33, 38

Galileo, 19, 60, 68
Gandhi, Mahatma, 48
Garibaldi, Giuseppe, 74
Gaylor, Anne Nicol, 18, 36, 37, 133, 137
Geneva, 5, 20, 21, 66, 88
Germany, 20, 25–27, 30, 41, 59, 65, 103, 109, 111, 115–17, 148, 162
Gibbon, Edward, 54; *The Decline and Fall of the Roman Empire*, 80, 123
Gilderhus, Mark: *History and Historians*, 74
Ginsburg, Carlo: *The Cheese and the Worms*, 128
Glover, John: *Humanity*, 133–35, 137–38, 149
Goldhagen, Daniel: *Hitler's Willing Executioners*, 138–40
Goldwater, Barry, 54
Gottlieb, Anthony, 159
Gould, Stephen Jay, 67
Gray, Charles, 115, 117–18
Grayling, A. C., 2, 164
Grobman, Alex, 152–53, 154
Guicciardini, Francesco, 121

Harris, Sam, 23, 31, 32, 33, 36, 41, 49, 51, 52, 53, 55, 71, 72, 80, 87, 90, 91, 107, 115, 132, 133–35, 137, 138, 142, 144–46, 148, 149, 158, 160, 161, 165; on Christianity, 19, 50, 71, 85, 86, 88, 91, 108, 109, 156; *The End of Faith*, 1, 12, 16, 88, 132, 156–57, 163; as historian, 1, 6, 10–11, 13, 31, 43, 47–48, 49–50, 57, 67, 138, 169; on Hitler, 28, 133, 135; on the Holocaust, 18–19, 39; on Islam, 56, 144, 145, 146–47; *Letter to a Christian Nation*, 88; *The Moral Landscape*, 70; on moral progress, 50–52, 55–56, 69, 70, 164; on Stalin, 11

Hawthorne, Nathaniel, 21
Hedges, Chris, 146–47
Henry IV. *See under* France
Herodotus, 120
Heschel, Abraham, 22
Hess, Rudolf, 16, 134
Hexter, J. H., 5, 131, 152
Hilberg, Raul, 139
Himmler, Heinrich, 27, 134
historicism, 82, 123, 124, 127, 130
Hitchens, Christopher, 2, 10, 13–14, 15, 33, 36, 41, 47, 50, 53, 57, 72, 86, 87, 88, 98, 105, 109, 116–17, 136, 142, 147, 148, 149, 155, 163; on Christianity, 20; on the Enlightenment, 45–47, 64, 70, 119; *God Is Not Great*, 1, 157–60; as historian, 6, 11, 22, 23, 31, 32, 43, 48, 67, 145; on Hitler, 19, 110; on Islamofascism, 146; on Martin Luther King, 22, 48; on North Korea, 15; on religion, 32, 80, 144; on Stalin, 110; on totalitarianism, 19, 20, 21, 88
Hitler, Adolf, 9, 12, 15, 19, 21, 24, 27–30, 37–41, 43, 88, 116, 117–18, 126, 132, 134–35, 136, 137, 138, 142, 146, 151, 160–61, 167; and the Catholic Church, 16, 20, 26, 27, 133; and Christianity, 20, 26, 27, 109, 110, 162; and the Holocaust, 16, 28, 38, 141; ideology of, 16, 20, 39, 41, 133
Holocaust, 3, 5, 16, 18–20, 27–28, 38–39, 40–41, 77, 86, 109, 116, 133–34, 139–41, 152–54, 163, 167; denial of, 117–19, 136, 167. *See also* Institute for Historical Review
Holy Roman Empire, 58, 59, 78, 89–90, 97, 101, 103, 107; Charles V, 90, 101, 103; Frederick I, 97, 107; Frederick II, 97, 107; Henry IV, 95
Huddleston, Trevor, 22
Huguenots, 102, 103
humanism, 25, 89, 100, 101, 121, 122

Hume, David, 52, 54, 142
Hundred Years War (1337–1453), 108
Huntington, Samuel, 145
Huxley, T. H., 48, 53, 54, 68, 71, 142

Inquisition, 51–52, 85, 86, 105, 110, 111, 128, 150
Institute for Historical Review, 17, 116
Irving, David, 115–19, 136, 152
Islam, 1, 5, 56, 87, 96, 129, 144, 145, 146–47, 151, 154, 156, 160
Italy, 64–65, 92, 94, 97, 99, 100, 103, 105, 121, 128

Jefferson, Thomas, 54, 61, 62
Jews, 17, 21, 26–28, 50, 77, 86, 87–88, 96, 103, 109, 116, 120, 138–41, 151, 168. *See also* anti-Semitism; Holocaust

Kant, Immanuel, 52
Katyn Forest massacre, 30–31
Khrushchev, Nikita, 31, 32, 33, 40, 131
Kierkegaard, Soren, 50
Kim Jon Il, 12
King, Martin Luther, 4, 22, 47
Kinsley, Michael, 159
Koeder, Christian, 155–56
Koestler, Arthur: *Darkness at Noon*, 30
Kuhn, Thomas, 66
Kulturkampf, 74

Ladurie, Emmanuel Le Roy: *Montaillou*, 128
Langer, Walter C., 126
Lea, H. C., 111
League of the Militant Godless, 10, 151
Lears, Jackson, 143–46, 165
Lefebrve, Leo, 37
Lenin, Vladimir, 9–10, 28, 32, 131, 150, 160–61
Lipstadt, Deborah, 115–18, 136, 152; *Denying the Holocaust*, 117
Livy, Titus, 120
Locke, John, 60, 61

Louis XIV. *See under* France
Luther, Martin, 87–89, 101, 102, 109, 110, 122, 126

Machiavelli, Nicola, 100, 121
Madison, James, 55, 61, 62
Manchester, William, 89; *A World Lit Only by Fire*, 81–84, 88
Mao Zedong, 151
Marx, Karl, 52, 53, 63, 125–26
Marxism, 10, 12, 29, 32, 34, 37, 40, 126, 128, 132, 137, 141–42, 160–62
Mattingly, David, 143
Mencken, H. L., 15
Merritt, Stephanie, 157
Middle Ages, 5, 6, 47–48, 67, 70, 78, 80, 81, 82, 85, 87, 94–95, 104, 107, 108, 110, 121–22, 138
Mussolini, Benito, 23–25, 29, 110, 146; and Ethiopian War, 24; and Lateran Accords, 24. *See also* fascism
My Lai massacre, 134

Napoleon Bonaparte, 46, 62, 64, 74
Naudé, Beyers, 22
Nazis, 5, 14, 19, 20, 23, 26, 29, 30, 31, 39, 41, 43, 115, 117, 134, 135, 136, 138, 139, 140; and the Catholic Church, 20, 136; and Christianity, 39, 41, 135, 138, 141; and eugenics, 27–28, 38, 39, 141, 145; ideology of, 27, 38, 148, 163; and religion, 38, 41, 134
Newton, Isaac, 60, 61
Niemoller, Martin, 21, 26
Nietzsche, Friedrich, 52, 53, 134, 135, 162
North Korea, 5, 14–15

Orr, H. Allen, 157
Orwell, George, 14, 19

Paine, Thomas, 54, 142
Palmer, R. R.: *The Age of the Democratic Revolution*, 62

papacy, 14, 19, 24, 28, 62, 78, 89, 90, 97, 99, 102, 107, 108, 112, 121, 122; Alexander III, 77; Boniface VIII, 97; and concordat with Germany, 26, 136; Gregory I, 92; Gregory VII, 78, 95; and the Holocaust, 28; Innocent III, 85, 86, 96, 97, 111–12; Innocent X, 58; Julius II, 100; Leo X, 74; Leo XIII, 74; Martin V, 97; Nicholas V, 100; Paul III, 102; Paul IV, 110; Pius VI, 72; Pius VII, 51; Pius IX, 64, 67; Pius XII, 20, 26, 28; Urban II, 95–96
Pascal, Blaise, 50, 142, 150
Pauley, Bruce: *Hitler, Stalin, and Mussolini*, 46
Petrarch, Francesco, 108
Pfaff, William, 145
Pinker, Steven, 2, 145–46, 163, 164–66; *The Better Angels of Our Nature*, 164
political religion, 41, 134
Pol Pot, 12, 142, 160
positivism, 47, 125, 144, 145, 153, 165
postmodernism, 130, 146
Prohibition, 55, 71
Protestantism, 21, 26, 27, 55, 57, 58, 62–64, 72, 74, 87–90, 102–3, 109, 110, 122, 124, 156, 162
Prussia, 59, 64, 124
Puritans, 90, 102

Radzinksy, Edward: *Stalin*, 34–35
Ranke, Leopold von, 122, 124, 153
Reformation, 47, 57, 82, 89, 100, 108, 109, 121, 142
Renaissance, 47, 65, 67, 80, 82, 99, 100, 108, 109, 121, 142
Richelieu, Cardinal, 72
Ridell, Mary, 158–59
Robespierre, Maximilien, 45–46, 62
Robinson, Marilynne, 71
Roman Empire, 58, 79, 80–81, 83, 85, 91–93, 123, 142
Romero, Oscar, 14

Roosevelt, Franklin Delano, 27
Rosenberg, Alex: *The Atheist's Guide to Reality*, 83
Rosenberg, Alfred: *The Myth of the Twentieth Century*, 27
Ruse, Michael, 78
Russian Orthodox Church, 9–10, 14, 29, 31, 33–37, 40

Scientific Revolution, 57, 60, 68, 69, 90, 143
Servetus, Michael, 88
Service, Robert: *Stalin*, 56, 150, 151
Seven Years War, 59
Shapin, Steven: *The Scientific Revolution*, 69
Shea, William R., 68
Shermer, Michael, 151–52, 166; and Alex Grobman, *Denying History*, 153–54
Singer, Peter, 49
Smith, Richard E, 18, 133, 137
Snyder, Timothy: *Bloodlands*, 43
Social Darwinism, 15, 39, 40, 135, 144, 165
Solzhenitsyn, Alexander, 149
South Africa, 22, 88, 159
Soviet Union, 38; religious policies of, 19, 29, 32–38, 131, 161; in World War II, 31, 34, 35, 40, 126
Spain, 21, 58, 90, 95, 103; Civil War (1936–39), 23, 29; Ferdinand and Isabella, 103, 111; Inquisition, 85, 103, 111; Philip II, 126
Spengler, Oswald, 128–29
Spinoza, Baruch, 54
Stalin, Josef, 12, 15, 22, 28, 30, 33, 43, 110, 111–12, 133, 134, 137, 141, 148; ideology of, 16, 132, 161; and Marxism, 12, 32, 142, 161; religious policies of, 14, 29, 31, 34–38, 72, 131, 150, 151; and the Russian Orthodox Church, 4, 9–11, 14, 29, 31, 40–41
Stenger, Victor, 2, 32–36, 39, 41, 67, 73–74, 77, 85–86, 107, 111–12, 144,

Stenger (*continued*)
151, 161, 169; *The New Atheism*, 32–36, 39, 67, 73–74
Stephens, Mitchell: *Imagine There's No Heaven*, 160–61
Suetonius, 120
Sun Myung Moon, 15

theocracy, 19, 95, 107
Thirty Years War (1618–48), 58, 72, 77, 86, 111; Peace of Westphalia (1648), 58, 59
Thucydides, 120
Toland, John, 16, 17–18, 116, 150, 152; *Hitler*, 16, 133; *Infamy: Pearl Harbor and Its Aftermath*, 17
Torquemada (Grand Inquisitor), 88
Tosh, John, 43, 130–31, 152, 153; *The Pursuit of History*, 43
totalitarianism, 4, 5, 14, 15, 18, 19, 20, 21, 24, 26, 28, 36, 42, 88, 109–10, 134
Tutu, Desmond, 22

Ukraine, 29, 43, 141

Valla, Lorenzo, 121–22
Vatican. *See* papacy

Voltaire, 48, 52, 61, 122, 142
Von Papen, Franz, 25

Walsh, W. H., 74
War of the Spanish Succession, 59
Washington, George, 61
Watson, Peter: *The Age of Atheists*, 162–64
Weikart, Richard: *From Darwin to Hitler*, 48
Weinberg, Steven, 2, 147–49
Westphalia, Peace of, 58–59
White, Andrew Dixon, 67, 68; *History of the Warfare of Science and Theology*, 66, 147
Wieseltier, Leon, 166
Wilberforce, Samuel, 64
William of Ockham, 98–99
witch hunts, 4, 51, 88
World War I, 23, 128, 134, 135, 144, 163
World War II, 10, 18, 28, 31, 34–35, 40, 115, 126

Young, G. M., 130

Zwingli, Ulrich, 102

The manufacturer's authorised representative in the EU is Springer Nature Customer Service Centre GmbH, Europaplatz 3, 69115 Heidelberg, Germany. If you have any concerns regarding our products, please contact ProductSafety@springernature.com

Printed and bound by CPI Group (UK) Ltd, Croydon, CR0 4YY
23/03/2026
02076673-0010